Correctional Law
for the
Correctional Officer,

5th Edition

William C. Collins, J.D.

Mission of the American Correctional Association

The American Correctional Association provides a professional organization for all individuals and groups, both public and private, that share a common goal of improving the justice system.

American Correctional Association Staff

Harold W. Clarke, President
James A. Gondles, Jr., CAE, Executive Director
Gabriella Daley Klatt, Director, Communications and Publications
Alice Heiserman, Manager of Publications and Research
Jeannelle Ferreira, Associate Editor
Shoshana Frishberg, Intern
Ryan Bounds, Intern
Xavaire Bolton, Graphics and Production Associate
Cover Design by Xavaire Bolton

Printed in the United States of America by Versa Press, Inc. East Peoria, IL.

This publication may be ordered from:
American Correctional Association
206 N. Washington St, Suite 200
Alexandria, VA 22314
For information on publications and videos available from ACA, contact our worldwide web home page at: www.aca.org/store or call (800) 222-5646 ext. 0129

Library of Congress Cataloging-in-Publication Data

Collins, William C., 1944-Correctional law for the correctional officer / William C. Collins. – 5th ed. p. cm. Includes index. ISBN 978-1-56991-321-5
1. Correctional law–United States. 2. Prisoners–Legal status, laws, etc.–United States. 3. Correctional personnel–Legal status, laws, etc.–United States. I. Title.
KF9728.C654 2010   344.7303'5–dc22   2010011172

Contents

Foreword

What separates the United States from totalitarian nations and countries with repressive governments is that in our country, our leaders follow the rule of law. This is also what makes our correctional systems different from those in many other countries — we are guided by our laws and not by the politics or impulses of governmental leaders. Laws are not static. They can change based on court decisions. The fifth edition of this best-selling book outlines and discusses the laws relevant to corrections.

The author, William Collins, a well-respected lawyer and expert on correctional law, provides guidance to correctional officers and others working in corrections so they understand their rights and the rights of inmates. *Correctional Law for the Correctional Officer* is an excellent addition to an academy's training curriculum or college introductory course. It is easy to read and serves as a quick reference for information that correctional officers need to perform their jobs within the law.

Correctional officers play a proud role in our law enforcement community. They are the professional backbone of our institutions and programs. As such, the better educated and trained our officers are means the better our facilities and programs operate, and the more successful we are at accomplishing our mission. The American Correctional Association (ACA) offers a professional certification program for correctional officers. Attaining certification means that the individual has achieved an exemplary level of competence and professionalism. Details on this program are available on our Web site at www.aca.org/certification.

Of course, we hope everyone reading this book will decide to become an ACA member, if they are not already members. Individual memberships are purposely inexpensive so that students and officers can afford to join and participate in the activities of the largest correctional association in the world. Membership information also is available on our Web site at www.aca.org or by calling (800) 222-5646, ext. 0129.

James A. Gondles, Jr., CAE
Executive Director
American Correctional Association

Chapter 1:
Introduction

We designed this book for the correctional officer. It describes, in a general way, many of the legal issues that the officer may face while working in corrections. Many of these issues relate to inmates, but some also focus on the officer and the officer's rights.

This volume does not address legal issues that may arise in juvenile institutions or programs; while a great deal of litigation has focused on adult institutions, relatively few lawsuits have been filed about conditions or practices in juvenile facilities. However, many of the fundamental principles discussed here apply to juvenile facilities and programs, including provision of medical care and avoidance of excessive force.

No one working in corrections can avoid dealing with legal issues from time to time. Legal rules govern much of what goes on in a prison or jail today. These may arise from state or federal statutes or state and federal constitutions. Courts may hold both agencies and officers accountable for violating these rules. We hope that this handbook will increase understanding of the role of law and the courts in corrections.

The Role of the Correctional Officer

The correctional officer has outgrown simply providing custody. The individual officers can affect the inmates lives. Some researchers believe the line officer is the most influential correctional employee in an inmate's life. The line officer is in a critical position to assist with the positive changes expected of the inmate.

Officers are responsible for carrying out the policies and rules of the correctional agency. The extent to which an institution abides by its own rules (and in turn complies with the requirements of statutes and the U.S. Constitution and state constitutions) depends a great deal on the correctional officer. The officers who know and follow the rules are unlikely to violate inmates' rights. A maverick officer who thinks nothing of ignoring agency rules and policies invites litigation.

Some Information about Lawsuits

The plaintiff is the person who files a lawsuit. The defendant is the person against whom the suit is filed.

Inmates typically file three types of lawsuits. We will discuss each of them. Civil rights claims directly concern the institution; sometimes they concern individual officers. The second type of claim challenges the inmate's conviction or sentence and does not concern the institution or officers. This type of suit is called a habeas corpus petition. The third type of claim, tort suits, seek damages based on someone's alleged negligence. These suits are brought in state court.

There are two types of civil rights claims. One attacks general policies, practices, or conditions. This type of suit often does not directly challenge any individual officers' actions, although its outcome may affect the officers' jobs. The other type of claim directly attacks actions (or failure to take actions) often claiming to follow the policies and procedures of the institution in a way that violated the rights of the inmate.

Policies and procedures, post orders, and other written job directives tell an officer what is expected. These are the best sources of law since they often are written to comply with statutory or constitutional requirements.

The Role and Function of the Courts

Courts play a unique role in our government and the criminal justice system. Like police and correctional agencies, courts play an active role in controlling crime, determining guilt or innocence, and imposing sentence. Courts also adjudicate civil (non-criminal) claims between private parties. However, courts also must perform a separate and distinct function: adjudicating whether government agencies or their employees have failed to abide by the requirements of the U.S. Constitution, or similar requirements of state constitutions.

The courts are like referees. They stand between the government and the individual to ensure that both play by the rules of the game. If they fail to decide questions, the game can get out of control. The Constitution provides basic rules. It is the duty of the courts to apply the Constitution to particular factual situations.

The U.S. Constitution and some state constitutions contain provisions designed to limit the power of government over individuals. These provisions contain, in broad language, the fundamentals of freedom. All of us accept these in their general and abstract form. There is probably near-universal agreement that we should have free speech, that a person accused of a crime should have an attorney, that the state should not inflict cruel and unusual punishments, and that people in similar circumstances should be treated equally by the government.

The courts, however, have the difficult task of applying these abstract principles to specific factual situations. The courts must decide what is a cruel and unusual punishment, when people are not being treated equally, or when the government may limit an inmate's religious practice. These are difficult decisions. Courts can act only when an individual asks them to decide a controversy by filing a lawsuit. However, when asked, the court cannot say, "That is too hard a question" or "I don't want to decide it now." In addition, courts must put the reasons for their decision in writing for all to examine.

The courts have recognized that sometimes, the interest of the government is so great that the rights of the individual must be narrowed. Thus, even though the Constitution says that Congress shall make no law abridging the freedom of speech, freedom of speech does not give someone the right to falsely yell "Fire!" in a crowded theater. Moreover, the First Amendment does not prohibit laws against perjury (telling lies under oath). Courts must balance the interest of the government and the interest of the individual, although this is a difficult and imprecise task.

Enforcement of some constitutional rules may make the tasks of a correctional institution more difficult. New rules may temporarily make it more difficult to retain control of offenders. However, this country has aspirations and goals beyond simply maintaining rigid control over those convicted of crime. We must give priority to fairness, justice, and respect for individual dignity.

Many people ask, "How can courts change their mind and rule one way one day and one way the next?" The answer is that all law changes. The demands of the Constitution are both general and flexible. What is cruel and unusual punishment today might not have been so in earlier times. The interests of the government also change as times change. For decades, the Supreme Court has interpreted the Constitution as a document with an evolving meaning. It is not locked into what judges now might think it may have meant in 1789. If it did, we would still have public whippings. The concept of court "precedent" generally requires a court to follow its prior rulings, but there are situations that allow a court to change its mind.

"How can one federal court rule one way on an issue on the same day another federal court elsewhere in the country rules the opposite way?" Judges look at history, at other court decisions, at the mood and temper of the times, and at what rule seems reasonable. Two judges reasonably can come to different answers on such questions, the same as two correctional officers will differ as to the most effective way to deal with an inmate under their supervision. Our judicial system is like a triangle, with the U.S. Supreme Court at the top. Thus, the Nebraska court can say what the law is, but its ruling affects only Nebraska, not Indiana. In the federal courts, an appeal can go to one of the twelve circuit courts whose rulings apply only to the states in that circuit. Supreme Court rulings, of course, apply to everyone. Thus, until the Supreme Court decides an issue, there may be inconsistent rulings in the lower courts.

Courts began to be involved with correctional issues in the late 1960s. For a number of years after that, controversy centered on the relationship of courts and corrections. After nearly four decades of court oversight, much of this controversy has died away. The courts have established an increasing number of fundamental principles, reducing confusion among both correctional administrators and courts as to precisely what the rules of the game are. We now recognize that inmates have certain rights and that officers also do. Many courts have become more conservative in their approach to civil rights and are more apt to rule in favor of the institution than the inmate.

Nevertheless, some changes in correctional law will continue simply because laws change. While the change may not be as rapid as it was during the 1970s, inmates and staff will still present disputes to the courts for resolution. Some of those case results will change the way correctional programs and facilities operate.

Chapter 2:
A Short History of the
Courts and Corrections

"I'll sue you!"

For someone entering the field of corrections in 2010, court involvement with correctional programs, inmate lawsuits or threatened lawsuits, and the concept of "inmate rights" may seem like an annoying but still routine fact. However, it has not always been this way. A few people still working in corrections can remember when court involvement was simply unheard of, and wardens or jail administrators were the final arbiters of "inmate rights."

Since about 1970, litigation—or the threat of litigation—has changed the way corrections does business. It is hard to find a part of inmate-related institutional operations which has not been the subject of a lawsuit or court order.

Inmates are not the only ones filing lawsuits in corrections. Increasingly, employment-related issues are "legal issues." These include employee discipline, discrimination, workplace safety, accommodations for employees with disabilities, and other issues. This change reflects the growing litigiousness (inclination to take issues to court) of American society.

The history of corrections and the courts can be divided into the following three eras:

1. The *hands-off era* was a time when courts simply would not respond to inmate claims. This period began to wane in the middle to late 1960s.

2. The *hands-on era* saw greatly increased court involvement with the operation of correctional institutions. This period ran from the demise of the hands-off period through most of the 1970s.

3. The *one-hand-on, one-hand-off era* saw a reduction of court intervention, caused by a series of decisions from the U.S. Supreme Court. These

decisions generally embraced the idea that inmates are protected by the Constitution. This period began in the 1980s and continues today.

The Hands-Off Era

For example, during the hands-off era, an Alaska court looked at conditions in a federal jail in Anchorage in 1951. The ancient wood frame jail housed up to forty inmates in a room that allowed less than nineteen square feet per inmate. Most of the floor space was consumed by bunks, tables, and benches. There were only twenty bunks for the forty inmates. There was no recreational capacity. Youths as young as sixteen were housed in the room. Health hazards existed due to the lack of ventilation, crowded conditions, and a single toilet and shower. Heat came from an old-fashioned coal-burning stove located in the room, which presented an obvious fire hazard. There was only a single exit, and an emergency exit could not have been added.

The judge said the room was not fit for human habitation and endorsed a description of the facility as a "fabulous obscenity." Although shocked by the conditions, the court refused to find an Eighth Amendment (cruel and unusual punishment) violation, noting that as bad as the conditions in the jail were, they were better than the conditions that soldiers fighting in the Korean War had to endure. The court also could find no relief that it could grant, short of simply releasing the inmates.[1]

Many courts justified not getting involved with correctional cases on the basis that judges knew nothing about running a correctional facility; therefore, the court should defer to the decisions made by wardens or others responsible for running prisons or jails. Federal courts also were reluctant to get involved in issues of state or local government out of concerns over *federalism*, a concept that holds that federal courts, if at all possible, should avoid interfering in state or local government activities.

During and before the 1960s, enormous discretion was left to correctional administrators about how their facilities were run. Court oversight, common today, did not exist. While state law set some outside limits, the courts imposed relatively little control on the day-to-day operation of a prison or jail because typically, no one outside the correctional agency had any responsibility for oversight. Even within a department of corrections, typically there was little centralized control. In many cases, "the law" within an institution was set—and enforced—by the warden or by individual officers in the cellblock.

As long as the lid was kept on a prison, the public seemed to care little about what went on in the facility. A riot or scandal might call attention to a prison from time to time, but generally, there was no active, regular review of prison practices or conditions.

The lack of public attention contributed to the physical and operational deterioration of many facilities. Funds to maintain or remodel old, worn-out institutions were hard to obtain, since funding sources such as legislatures or county commissions saw little political reason to pour tax money into prison or jail improvements.

This same political reality tended to keep operational appropriations low, so staff salaries stayed low, and little if any money was available for training. Correctional officers now often must attend and pass hundreds of hours of training in specialized academies before being fully qualified to work. By comparison, a survey taken in the mid-1960s showed more than 40 percent of the state correctional systems did not even require a high school diploma for entry-level starting correctional officers.[2] Wardens often were appointed based on politics, not professionalism or experience.

This lack of almost any regular external oversight, combined with poorly trained staff and a lack of professional leadership, allowed serious abuses to develop in facilities across the country. Lawyers began to bring examples of these abuses to the courts.

The 1960s was an era of civil rights attention and reform. During the 1950s and 1960s, courts, particularly federal courts, increasingly were involved in large reform lawsuits. Public attention focused on many groups outside the mainstream of American culture, and efforts were made to improve the lot of those groups.

With this heightened concern for civil rights in general, it was inevitable that conditions and practices in correctional facilities would receive attention. Unfortunately, facilities and their management often were very unprepared for such scrutiny. Frequently, administrators could not defend the practices or conditions that were the subject of suits as appropriate under any theory of modern penology. Administrators and their lawyers often reacted to potential court intervention by ignoring the facts of the case or the legal theories underlying the case and instead argued that the court had no business "meddling" in the operation of the prison or jail. This sort of emotional response was increasingly unsuccessful.

The End of the Hands-off Era

A combination of factors led to the end of the hands-off era. Civil rights issues were coming to the courts from many directions. The mood of the country favored reform and improving conditions for the less fortunate, and many young lawyers were interested in working with reform cases. However, more than anything else, the facts of the cases that got to court were what led to the end of the hands-off period.

1. As late as 1965, the Arkansas prison system allowed whipping. The person doing the whipping made the decision whether to whip an inmate. Supposedly, lashes were limited to ten lashes per offense. In some cases, staff allowed inmate-trusties to whip other inmates. The whipper administered the whippings on the bare buttocks of the inmates. Also, in Arkansas, the infamous "Tucker telephone" administered electric shocks to inmates' genitals as a form of punishment. Inmates received these sorts of punishments without any hearing to determine if the inmate had violated a rule.[3]

Case Study: The "Courts Shouldn't Meddle" Defense

In 1966, a group of black inmates filed suit in federal court in Alabama attacking state laws that required racial segregation in state and local correctional facilities. In an era when similar equal protection challenges to racial segregation in all types of government activities filled the courts, the defendants' only response to the suit was to argue that racial segregation in prisons or jails was a "matter of routine prison security and discipline and (therefore) was not within the scope of permissible inquiry by the courts." The court rejected this defense, found the practices unconstitutional, and ordered the facilities desegregated. The Supreme Court upheld the lower court decision. *Washington v. Lee*, 263 F.Supp. 327 (M.D. Ala., 1966), affirmed 88 S.Ct. 994 (1968).

2. The first overall prison conditions case also came from Arkansas. Armed inmates—trusties—guarded other inmates. Only two correctional officers were on duty at night in a prison holding nearly 1,000 men. Abuses of the trusty system—bribery, extortion, smuggling, and so forth—were common.

Most inmates in the Arkansas prisons were housed in dormitories. Placement in a particular unit was based on race (blacks were segregated) and rank in the institution. No free-world staff entered the dorms at night. Inmate "floor-walkers" were responsible for keeping order, but were ineffective. It was common for inmates to creep from one bunk to another to stab an enemy. Rape was common, and at night, the floorwalkers would not interfere with a sexual assault.

The trusties also commonly interfered with access to medical services. Sanitation in the kitchen was described as "deplorable." The judge who reviewed overall conditions in this system called it "a dark and evil world completely alien to the free world, a world that is administered by criminals under unwritten codes and customs completely foreign to free-world culture."[4]

The following quotation ended the opinion and captured the essence of the prisoners' rights movement. Today, we know there are no excuses that can justify a prison that does not meet the requirements of the U.S. Constitution.

> Let there be no mistake in the matter; the obligation of [Arkansas officials] to eliminate existing unconstitutionalities does not depend upon what the Legislature may do, or upon what the Governor may do, or, indeed, upon what [the officials] may actually be able to accomplish. If Arkansas is going to operate a Penitentiary System, it is going to have to be a system that is countenanced by the Constitution of the United States.[5]

3. In Alabama, a suit was filed dealing with medical care. Inmates there routinely handled both treatment (!) and records. In one situation, a maggot-infested wound went twenty days before anyone did anything to change the dressings or clean and disinfect it. An incontinent patient was kept sitting on a bench so he would not soil the bedclothes. His condition caused him to fall a lot; eventually his leg had to be amputated. Sanitation in the medical department was poor. There was a serious shortage of qualified doctors.[6]

4. In another case, death row inmates were locked in their six-by-nine cells all but fifteen minutes a day. This regimen lasted as long as the inmate remained on death row, up to nine years in one case. This led the court to order out-of-the-cell exercise and led to later cases requiring outdoor exercise several times a week.[7]

The courts that heard these early cases were reluctant to abandon the hands-off approach, but the facts the inmates and their lawyers presented clearly shocked them. The defendants—those accountable for running the facilities—offered little or no responsible justification for their actions, other than perhaps to plead a lack of funding. It was clear that unless the courts intervened in some way, the shocking, violent, and inhumane practices would continue. Faced with the choice of allowing the conditions and practices to continue or intervening to try to prevent them from continuing, courts began to intervene, and the hands-off era became history.

The Hands-on Era

The hands-on era began with courts responding to the sorts of shocking situations described. Many cases dealt with conditions, but others dealt with operational issues such as due process in disciplinary hearings and under what circumstances inmate religious freedoms could be restricted.

The courts' sudden involvement with correctional issues created a great deal of controversy among correctional administrators, some of which continues today. Several factors compounded the controversy. Courts never had looked over corrections' shoulder before. Because correctional law as a separate area of legal concern was "invented" around 1970, there were no court *precedents* (earlier cases establishing fundamental principles in correctional law) to guide the courts or prepare institutional administrators or their lawyers to defend their positions. A number of lawyers around the country aggressively began litigating on behalf of inmates, trying to use the courts almost as super-legislative bodies to create and enforce new correctional policy in all sorts of areas.

Case Study: Rehabilitation Programs — Not a Right, But...

Courts consistently agreed with the general principle that there was no constitutional right to rehabilitation or rehabilitation programs for inmates. Yet, sometimes courts ordered the development of such programs.

One court reasoned that inmates had a right not to be housed in a setting that was counterproductive to rehabilitation, in conditions that could cause degeneration. Because the New Hampshire State Prison conditions involved pervasive idleness, only make-work jobs, and very few meaningful vocational or educational programs, the court felt the prison was creating unconstitutional degenerative conditions, counterproductive to rehabilitation.

Given those conclusions, the court then ordered the institution to provide each inmate with the opportunity to participate in educational and recreational programs and to learn a skill marketable in New Hampshire. *Laaman v. Helgemoe*, 437 F.Supp. 269 (D.N.H., 1977).

It is very unlikely that the courts would issue such an order today.

Given the lack of precedent, the courts created new rights, such as the right to exercise, and these rights grew rapidly. Probably the first case where exercise was an issue involved the extreme situation of death row inmates mentioned earlier. They lived for years in six-by-nine cells with little natural light and were allowed out of their cells for only fifteen minutes per day. The court found these conditions to be cruel and unusual punishment and ordered that the inmates be provided outdoor exercise.[8] No real discussion occurred on the effect of the lack of exercise on inmates, nor did anyone consider whether indoor exercise could have met the inmates' needs.

Soon the "right" that had been created for death row inmates locked in their cells twenty-three hours and forty-five minutes per day was applied to jail inmates.[9] Then, another court discussed the "fundamental" right to exercise and the importance of inmates being able to see the open sky, sun, and clouds.[10]

Therefore, in a matter of only a few years, courts had gone from never having talked about inmate exercise rights, to finding a need for exercise in an extreme situation, to deciding exercise was a fundamental right somehow related to being able to see the sun and perhaps feel the wind in one's face. The variation in the amount of exercise courts require shows the confusion created by this sort of approach. Some said inmates had to exercise an hour per day every day. Others said an hour per day for three-to-five days per week was sufficient. Most courts came to recognize that a few days without exercise would not violate a right. Still others were less concerned about the outdoor aspect than being sure the exercise space was large enough (and perhaps equipped) for large muscle exercise. It was obvious that year-round outdoor exercise was not possible in much of the country, where weather conditions would not permit it.

The Supreme Court's two major conditions-of-confinement decisions somewhat resolved this confusion. The Court said the key question about the adequacy of conditions was the effect they had on inmates.[11] Now, a condition or practice (such as the lack of exercise) must be shown to have a serious effect on inmates before it may be unconstitutional.

Other examples of the extent of court involvement during the decade of the 1970s include the following:

1. One court ordered that the prison daily diet must include "at least one fresh green vegetable, one fresh yellow vegetable, and serving of meat or protein-provided meat substitute." This requirement was reversed on appeal.[12]

11

2. A decision involving many conditions and practices at a new federal jail in New York City was more than fifty pages long. The district court required officials to allow pretrial detainees (but not convicted inmates) to be present during cell searches. The courts found double celling (placing two inmates in a cell designed for one) unconstitutional. Pretrial detainees were allowed to wear their own clothing or uniforms, but the court did not permit jail jumpsuits.[13]

Probably the most significant trends among lower courts during the 1970s were the assumption that double celling was automatically unconstitutional and the increased reliance on professional standards (such as those set by the American Correctional Association). Despite the controversy created by the sudden and dramatic involvement of the courts in corrections, one must wonder, in hindsight, if many of the problems the courts addressed would have been addressed and corrected in any other way had the courts maintained their hands-off approach.

The One-Hand-On, One-Hand-Off Era

The momentum the lower courts built up in corrections cases during the 1970s began to slow as the decade ended. The main reason for this slowing was the U.S. Supreme Court. It takes years for a case to get from a federal district court, through the court of appeals, to the Supreme Court. While the Supreme Court is asked to review many cases, it selects only a few for consideration— cases that the Court believes raise especially important legal issues. Since the concepts of correctional law and inmate rights barely had begun to develop in 1970, it is then not surprising that few cases or issues got to the Supreme Court before the late 1970s.

As correctional issues slowly found their way to the Court, another development was taking place: many of the liberal justices who made up the "Warren Court" of the 1950s and 1960s were retiring; they were replaced by more conservative justices. So, by the second half of the 1970s, a somewhat conservative Court awaited the correctional law cases that were coming to the Court for decision.

One of the first suggestions of the Court's conservatism came in a case in which the issue was whether a prison rule prohibiting an inmates' "labor union" violated the inmates' First Amendment rights of free speech and association.[14] The Court upheld the ban. Perhaps more significant than the immediate result was what the Court said about courts deferring to the judgment and concerns of prison officials: "It is enough to say that they have not been conclusively shown to be wrong in this view" (that an inmates' labor union would be a threat to security and order in the prison). According to the court, officials did not have to prove their concerns were valid. Instead, those attacking the concerns had to prove they were wrong or exaggerated. The Court reemphasized this principle in a 2003 case involving an attack on various restrictions a department of corrections had placed on visiting: "The burden, moreover, is not on the State to prove the validity of prison regulations but on the prisoner to disprove it."[15]

Nevertheless, the most dramatic indication of the direction the Court wanted to go with correctional issues came in the case of *Bell v. Wolfish*,[16] probably the single most important correctional case the Court ever has decided. *Bell* was a major crowding/conditions of confinement case that involved a new federal jail in Manhattan. The district court had found many conditions and practices in the facility unconstitutional. Parts, but not all, of the district court's order were appealed to the court of appeals, which upheld some portions and reversed others. Lawyers took some of the issues from the court of appeals' decision to the Supreme Court. Though the case that got to the Supreme Court was much narrower than the case decided by the district court, it still contained some very important issues, the most significant of which was the question of whether double-celling inmates violated the Constitution.

The Court specifically rejected the idea that single celling was constitutionally required. The Court said there was "no one-man, one-cell principle lurking" in the Constitution and approved double-bunking in the jail under review.[17] The Court said that factors such as the time out of the cell and the activities available to inmates were more important considerations than just the number of inmates in a cell. The Court also rejected correctional standards (such as American Correctional Association standards) as a measure of the Constitution.

The Court refused to hold that the presumption of innocence enjoyed by pretrial detainees somehow was relevant to judging the conditions of confinement in a jail. The Court criticized lower courts for becoming "enmeshed in the minutiae of prison operations." The case also approved rules that allow inmates to receive books or publications only from publishers (publishers-only rules) and a policy of strip-searching inmates after returning from contact visits.

Bell sent a message to lower courts that while inmates did enjoy constitutional rights, those rights were more subject to restriction than many courts had suggested. The Supreme Court repeated the "slow down" message in several due process cases. The Court ruled that transfers into administrative segregation were not inherently protected by the Fourteenth Amendment.[18] Nor did due process protect an inmate who was transferred from one prison to another, even if the transfer was over thousands of miles.[19] The latter half of the 1980s saw the Court state even more clearly that lower courts should defer to the judgment and concerns of prison officials.

In a series of cases, the Court set out a specific test for courts to evaluate cases that involved a conflict between an inmate's constitutionally protected interests and a legitimate interest of the institution. This test makes restrictions on inmates' constitutional rights easier to defend than under the approaches most lower courts had taken previously.

While the Supreme Court was telling lower courts to slow down and not substitute their judgment about how best to run a prison for the judgment of the persons hired and trained to do this difficult job, the level of professionalism in institutions was growing. Line staff became better trained and supervised. Carefully developed policies and procedures replaced "the seat of the pants" as a guide for making decisions. An increasing number of agencies worked to be formally accredited. Many states adopted jail standards and inspected jails for compliance with those standards. Institutions began to follow the now well-developed case law that existed for many areas of prison and jail operations. Thus, institutions were able to defend themselves better than they had in the early years of the inmate-rights movement.

The Supreme Court's conservative trend has become more pronounced into the twenty-first century.

Congress and Inmate Lawsuits: The Prison Litigation Reform Act (PLRA)

Perhaps the most significant single development in correctional law during the decade of the 1990s did not come from the courts defining a new inmate right or modifying an old one. The development came from the U.S. Congress in the form of the Prison Litigation Reform Act (PLRA).

Many have criticized the entire inmate-rights movement for resulting in inmates filing thousands upon thousands of lawsuits every year. Most of the cases are filed in federal district court and most are dismissed prior to trial in favor of defendants. Other criticism directed at federal courts was for taking an overly active role in controlling or directing actions of correctional agencies, and for becoming too "enmeshed in the minutiae of prison operations." [20]

Much has been written about inmates flooding the federal courts with lawsuits. While the numbers bear this out, they also reflect the huge increase in the total number of persons incarcerated in this country and raise other questions, as well. The following statistics come from *Inmate Litigation*, by Margo Schlanger, writing in the *Harvard Law Review* 116: 1555 (2003).

Inmate civil rights filings in federal courts increased from 2,267 in 1970 to more than 39,000 in 1995. At the same time, the total inmate populations (prison and jail) in the United States increased from about 357,000 to nearly 1.6 million. So, while the rate of civil rights filings per 1,000 inmates increased sharply from 1970-1980 (the "hands-on" era), the rate did not vary substantially between 1980 and 1995. Regardless of rates per 1,000 inmates and increasing total inmate populations, 39,000 lawsuits is still a large number.

Congress responded to criticisms of inmates filing too many meritless cases by passing the Prison Litigation Reform Act (PLRA), a package of laws that, among other things, makes it more difficult for inmates to file cases. The law also makes it somewhat easier for courts to dismiss cases and limits the power of the federal courts to enter relief against a prison after the court finds constitutional violations. The PLRA also makes it easier for correctional officials to terminate court orders entered against them.

We will discuss the details of the PLRA elsewhere in this book. However, in general terms, the PLRA makes it harder for inmates to file lawsuits in several ways. The most significant of these is the requirement that even indigent inmates must pay a full filing fee (through what amounts to a down payment and subsequent "EZ monthly payments"), despite their lack of funds. Previously, a court could waive the filing fee altogether.[21] Having to pay $350 to take a case to court has clearly deterred many inmates from filing civil rights claims.

Additionally, the PLRA creates a "three strikes and you're out" provision.[22] This section of the law says any inmate who has had three cases dismissed as frivolous, malicious, or which "fail to state a claim for which relief can be granted," is barred from filing any new cases without paying the full filing fee when the case is filed, unless the inmate alleges he is under "imminent danger of serious physical harm." Since a relatively small number of inmates file a large number of lawsuits, the three-strikes law is cutting off many "frequent filers" from getting to court.

PLRA also requires that inmates exhaust all administrative remedies (such as grievances and internal appeals) before filing a civil rights case.

If Congress wanted to reduce the number of cases inmates filed, it got its wish. According to testimony given by Professor Margo Schlanger before a Congressional Committee on November 8, 2007, in the decade following passage of the PLRA, the rate at which prisoners filed lawsuits dropped from 26 federal cases per 1,000 inmates in 1995 to 11 such cases in 2005. This amounts to a decline of nearly 60 percent![23] Inmate civil rights filings had risen every year from 1970 until passage of the PLRA. The dramatic, unprecedented decrease in filings can be attributed almost exclusively to the Prison Litigation Reform Act.

State by State Variations

The rate at which inmates file civil rights claims varies dramatically among states. In 1991, inmates in Iowa filed section 1983 suits at the rate of 129 suits per 1,000 inmates, while inmates in Rhode Island filed just over four per 1,000. Massachusetts inmates filed just under eight suits per 1,000 inmates. Seven years later, in 1998, Nevada inmates "led the league" by filing about 104 suits per 1,000 inmates while Iowa had dropped to less than 39 per 1,000. Rhode Island and Massachusetts inmates still filed suits at the lowest rate.[24]

What might explain such a twenty-fold difference between states? How much of prison or jail administrators' actions contribute to the rate at which inmates file lawsuits?

While inmates file many civil rights cases, they did not succeed very often. The Schlanger article (cited above) discussed a study of all federal district court cases that were terminated (not filed) by a judgment in 1995. Inmate civil rights cases were by far the largest of ten categories. More than 80 percent of the inmate cases were dismissed before trial in favor of the defendant. The next highest dismissal rate was 53 percent that the plaintiff voluntarily dismissed. The plaintiff voluntarily dismissed another 7 percent. Some of these were voluntarily dismissed because the case was settled in some informal way, so some of these may reflect an inmate "win." Six percent of the cases were formally settled; again, presumably indicating the inmate got something out of the lawsuit. Only 3 percent of the cases actually went to trial and the inmate won 10 percent of these.[25]

To summarize these numbers, if one perhaps generously assumes that all of the voluntary dismissals reflected a settlement that gave the inmate something and adds that to the other figures that reflect an inmate "win," inmates "won" something in only about 14 of every 100 cases. While the major aspects of the Prison Litigation Reform Act have been challenged as unconstitutional, courts have upheld all major aspects of the Act.

The Future of Court Intervention and Corrections

The era of expanding inmate rights is clearly over, replaced by a time of reduced court intervention in corrections. Almost every Supreme Court decision since the 1980s has trimmed back what lower courts have said about the rights of inmates. In some cases, the Supreme Court has even retreated from earlier decisions.

For example, in 1974, the Court at least appeared to say that inmates were entitled to due process protections when facing disciplinary charges for which they could be put in segregation (notice, a hearing, a limited right to call witnesses, and so forth).[28] Twenty-one years later, in 1995, the Court in *Sandin v. Conner* held no due process protections existed for a sentenced inmate facing a disciplinary sanction of thirty days in segregation.[29] In addition to "reinterpreting" what it said in 1974, the Court in the *Sandin* case also completely rejected its own interpretation of how lower courts should decide if due process protections applied to almost any decision a prison or jail might make which adversely affected an inmate.[30]

In 1996, the Court revisited a 1977 decision regarding access to the courts in *Lewis v. Casey*.[31] *Lewis* upheld the basic principles from the earlier case, that inmates have a constitutionally protected right of access to the courts and that prison officials have a duty to assist inmates in the preparation and filing of meaningful legal papers. At the same time, the court in *Lewis* reinterpreted how these principles should be applied. The result: it is considerably harder for an inmate to win an access to the courts case, especially if the inmate is claiming that law library resources were insufficient.

As noted in the previous section, the decision by Congress to pass the Prison Litigation Reform Act sets up barriers. Inmates must surmount them to get a case to court. Congress also attempted to put checks on the power of federal courts to oversee facilities found to be unconstitutional in some way.

Despite pressure for reduced court involvement with corrections, court oversight of many practices and conditions in jails and prisons will continue, and persons working in corrections, from the newest officer to the longtime warden, need to remain sensitive to the rights of inmates. Conditions of confinement will continue to be a major concern, as prison and jail populations continue to climb. While crowding is not necessarily unconstitutional, serious constitutional problems often are the product of crowding, as a soaring inmate population outstrips the ability of an institution to provide for the basic human needs of the inmates.

Courts in the future will be called upon to enforce existing rights in the areas of medical care and use of force. However, new issues will continue to emerge. Problems have arisen in recent years concerning sexual contact between staff and inmates. This is an unfortunate by-product of the growth of cross-gender work forces. The numbers of elderly inmates in prison will continue to grow substantially, bringing with them a huge increase in costs to provide necessary medical care. Older inmates may also be more vulnerable to exploitation by younger offenders.

Already visible in some states, state courts will continue to become more active in inmate cases. Where the federal courts are retreating from protection of inmate rights, litigators will reexamine state courts as a possible source of relief. State laws or constitutions can require more of corrections than does the federal Constitution. Increasingly, prison advocates will test state courts for their receptivity to inmate-rights issues.

Another development of recent years is staff's increased willingness to assert their legal rights through lawsuits against government agencies. Congress expanded the legal rights of persons with disabilities when it passed the Americans with Disabilities Act of 1990 (ADA). This sweeping law and its accompanying federal regulations provide protections for employees (and job applicants), inmates, and even for persons visiting correctional institutions. The ADA has been the source of numerous lawsuits affecting corrections. This is the subject of Chapter 12.

Reduction of court oversight, brings with it the seeds of potential problems later. The threat of lawsuits during the last twenty years contributed to correctional professionals becoming much more sensitive about understanding what legally they can and cannot do. If the threat of litigation subsides in many areas, the incentive to obey the law created by that threat may erode. If this occurs, serious abuses may increase. In a worst-case scenario, a few such gross abuses could come to the attention of the courts and trigger a resurrection of the hands-on era, with courts again seeing themselves as the only protection available to inmates.

To a large degree, whether this worst-case scenario occurs will depend on the professionalism of the men and women working in corrections. If they insist on doing their jobs in accordance with recognized professional standards and practices, there will be little reason for court involvement. However, if administrators abandon such benchmarks and allow facilities and individual staff to drift with little supervision or training, serious problems are likely to emerge and bring a new era of court intervention.

Of particular concern today are the tremendous budget problems plaguing state and local governments. Where budgets are slashed because there is no money and governments are unable or unwilling to raise taxes to generate more revenue, then all the professionalism staff can muster may not be enough to prevent serious deterioration in the quality of prison or jail operations.

Review Questions

1. What were the three periods or eras of court involvement with corrections?

2. List two factors that led to the courts first becoming involved with correctional issues.

3. What two major goals did Congress attempt to accomplish in passing the Prison Litigation Reform Act?

4. Is the Supreme Court requiring lower courts to show increased or decreased deference to the judgment of correctional officers and administrators?

Endnotes

[1] *Ex Parte Pickens*, 101 F.Supp. 285 (D. Alas., 1951).

[2] *Task Force Report: Corrections*, p. 181, President's Commission on Law Enforcement and Administration of Justice, 1967.

[3] *Jackson v. Bishop*, 404 F.2d 571 (8th Cir., 1968).

[4] *Holt v. Sarver*, 309 F.Supp. 362 (E.D. Ark., 1970).

[5] Id, at 385.

[6] *Newman v. Alabama*, 503 F.2d 1320 (5th Cir., 1974).

[7] *Sinclair v. Henderson*, 331 F.Supp. 1123 (D. La., 1971).

[8] *Sinclair v. Henderson*.

[9] *Taylor v. Sterret*, 334 F.Supp. 411 (N.D. Tex., 1972).

[10] *Rhem v. Malcolm*, 371 F.Supp. 594 (S.D.N.Y., 1974); 432 F.Supp. at 782.

[11] *Bell v. Wolfish*, 441 U.S. 529 (1979). *Rhodes v. Chapman*, 452 U.S. 337 (1981).

[12] *Smith v. Sullivan*, 563 F.2d 373 (5th Cir., 1977).

[13] U.S. ex rel. *Wolfish v. Levy*, 439 F.Supp. 114 (S.D.N.Y., 1977). Portions of this decision were later reversed in *Bell v. Wolfish*.

[14] *Jones v. North Carolina Prisoners' Labor Union*, 433 U.S. 119 (1977).

[15] *Overton v. Bazzetta*, 123 S.Ct. 2162 (2003).

[16] 441 U.S. 529 (1979).

[17.] 441 U.S. at 542.

[18.] *Hewitt v. Helms*, 103 S.Ct. 864 (1982).

[19.] *Olim v. Wakinekona*, 461 U.S. 238 (1983).

[20.] *Bell v. Wolfish*, 441 U.S. 520, 562 (1979).

[21.] 28 USC §1915 (b).

[22.] 29 USC §1915 (g).

[23.] Schlanger, Margo, 2003. *Harvard Law Review*, Vol 116, p 1555.

[24.] Schlanger, Table I.A, p. 1583.

[25.] Hanson, Roger A. and Henry W. K. Day. 1995. *Challenging the Conditions of Prisons and Jails: A Report on Section 1983 Litigation*, Office of Justice Programs.

[26.] Schlanger, Table II.A, p. 1594.

[27.] *Wolff v. McDonnell*, 4180 U.S. 539 (1974).

[28.] See *Hewitt v. Helms*, 459 U.S. 460 (1983).

[29.] *Sandin v. Conner*, 115 S.Ct. 2293 (1995).

[30.] *Lewis v. Casey*, 518 U.S. 343 (1996), *Bounds v. Smith*, 430 U.S. 817 (1977).

Chapter 3:
Types of Lawsuits Inmates File

Almost all litigation filed by inmates falls into one of three categories: (1) civil rights actions, in which the inmate claims a condition or practice of the institution violates a constitutional right, (2) habeas corpus actions, in which the inmate challenges the legality of being in custody at all, and (3) tort suits, in which an inmate claims he or she was damaged as the result of someone's negligence.

The Civil Rights Act

The overwhelming majority of lawsuits filed by offenders that involve correctional personnel are civil rights actions brought under a federal statute, 42 United States Code Section 1983, commonly known as the Civil Rights Act or "Section 1983." Congress passed the Civil Rights Act in 1871. It reads as follows:

> Every person who, under color of any statute, ordinance, regulation, custom, or usage, of any state or territory, subjects, or causes to be subject, any citizen of the United States or other person within the jurisdiction thereof to the deprivation of any rights, privileges, or immunities secured by the Constitution and laws, shall be liable to the party injured in an action at law, suit in equity, or other proper proceeding for redress.

The act was originally passed to address wrongs done by the Ku Klux Klan in the post-Civil War South. For decades, the law received little notice. The civil rights movement in the 1950s and 1960s "rediscovered" the act. It became the major vehicle for much of the civil rights litigation of that era. Subsequently, "Section 1983," as the act often is referred to, became commonly used in all forms of civil rights litigation, including the prisoners' rights movement that began in the late 1960s.

Civil rights suits typically are filed in federal district court, but can be filed in state court.

To have a legitimate claim under Section 1983 (in legal jargon, "to state a claim"), the plaintiff must establish that a person, acting under color of state law, caused a violation of constitutional rights or federal statutory rights. On establishing such a violation, the court can find the violator liable either for damages or for other forms of judicially ordered relief.

Defendants must be "Persons"

Civil rights actions only can be brought against persons. They cannot be brought directly against the state (or state agencies), since the state and its agencies are not considered persons. Interestingly, the Supreme Court has ruled that municipal corporations, such as cities and counties, are persons and can be sued directly in a civil rights action.[1] The "person" issue becomes important with regard to damages in Section 1983 suits. Since the state is not a person, the state cannot be sued directly for damages under Section 1983. However, units of local government can be and often are sued for damages, since they are now persons under Section 1983.

Color of State Law

As a general rule, suits can be brought only against government employees for actions arising out of their employment, in other words, employees acting "under color of state law." Thus, a civil rights action cannot be brought against an offender since the actions of the offender are not taken under color of state law. In a case brought by an inmate against a private doctor, who worked for the prison under a contract, the Supreme Court held that the doctor was still considered to be acting under color of state law.[2] Thus, the doctor was subject to possible liability under Section 1983. This case stands for the principle that employees of private prison companies are subject to suit under Section 1983.

Must Prove Violation of Constitution or Federal Statute

The action must establish a violation of a constitutional right (generally a right guaranteed by the Bill of Rights and/or the Fourteenth Amendment to the U.S. Constitution) or a violation of a federal statutory right. Violations of federal statutes rarely are alleged in correctional litigation because very few federal statutes protect inmates.

Personal Involvement

The general rule is that to be liable, a defendant actually must have in caused the constitutional violation. Liability may not be imposed simply because the defendant has some supervisory authority over the individual whose direct actions caused the violation. Under a legal doctrine known as *respondeat superior*, "let the master answer," liability can be imposed against an employee for the acts of an employee simply because of the employment relationship. The doctrine does not apply in Section 1983 lawsuits. In other words, in a 1983 action, the defendant must cause the injury to the plaintiff. We will discuss this respondeat superior doctrine later in this chapter.

Supervisory Liability

Section 1983 imposes liability when someone "causes one to be subject to" a constitutional violation. Courts may be asked to focus on this language to assess potential liability on supervisory personnel who did not directly participate in the challenged act or omission. Such cases often focus on one of two specific areas:

1. **Failure to Supervise.** Where a supervisory staff member has knowledge of a pattern of constitutionally offensive acts but fails to take remedial steps, liability may attach if the supervisor's actions or inactions can be said to be "deliberately indifferent" to the constitutional rights of the victim. An example of this might occur when a supervisor is aware of and apparently condones staff using excessive force against inmates.

The following is an example of a failure-to-supervise claim made against a first-level supervisor in a medium-sized jail.

> One evening in December 2002, Officer Leonard was under the supervision of Senior Officer Malone. Officer Leonard was so new to the job that he was still in his six-week on-the-job-training program required of all new officers. Lockdown in the jail was at 10 p.m. and any time a cell door was opened after that time, a note had to be entered in the shift log.
>
> Officer Leonard entered a female inmate's cell three times between 10 and 11 P.M., allegedly kissing her and trying to have sex with her. He performed oral sex on her the second time he entered the cell. While he told Officer Malone each time he went to the inmate's cell, he did not report entering the cell. Officer Malone raised no question about why a rookie officer would be going to a female inmate's cell three times in an hour when there was no apparent reason to do so.

Officer Malone said he had no idea Officer Leonard entered the cell, although there was a light panel directly in front of Officer Leonard's workstation that would have shown a red light every time the inmate's cell door was open. There was a factual disagreement over whether Officer Malone could see the inmate's cell from his workstation, but even the sheriff testified that one could see into the cells from the workstation.

On appeal, Officer Malone argued that he could not be liable because he subjectively did not know Officer Leonard was sexually assaulting the inmate. The court said that a supervisor need not have knowledge of the actual harm inflicted on the plaintiff to be liable in a section 1983 action, but could be liable if he acted with "deliberate, reckless indifference" to a substantial risk of serious harm. While the case came to the court of appeals before a trial and there were still unresolved disputes about key facts, the court said that if a jury believed the plaintiff's version of what happened, it could find Officer Malone deliberately indifferent to a substantial risk of serious harm to the inmate. Officer Malone knew a rookie officer made three visits to the woman's cell in less than an hour. He stayed at least five minutes on one of the visits. Officer Malone either knew the cell door was opened (because a red light went on in front of him) or was paying absolutely no attention to the light panel.[3]

This decision highlights the idea that supervisors cannot turn a blind eye to suspect behavior going on around them and thereby avoid possible liability. Officer Malone may not have known that Officer Leonard was sexually assaulting an inmate, but he was aware of suspicious behavior by his subordinate and did nothing in response to that behavior.

2. **Failure to Train.** If a failure to train is so serious as to reflect "deliberate indifference" to the constitutional rights of someone, the agency (but rarely, if ever, the supervisor) may be held liable.[3] This might occur if a supervisor assigned a new staff member to a constitutionally sensitive position knowing the person assigned did not have training in the constitutional issues involved.

For instance, suppose a correctional officer were assigned to supervise a housing unit without understanding that inmates have a constitutionally protected right to receive medical care. The officer unilaterally decides that a medical order that the inmate be given a lower bunk conflicts with his authority to make bunk assignments in the unit and requires the inmate to stay in an upper bunk. The inmate's medical condition becomes much worse as a result. The officer's actions could expose the supervisor to failure-to-train liability even though the supervisor was not directly involved in the actions of the officer.

Case Study: Tolerating Violence Leads to Supervisory Liability

The arrestee, who had attempted to shoot a police officer, was brought to the holding facility and beaten by several officers, even though supervisors were present during the beating. The inmate again was beaten that night, and the night supervisor did nothing to prevent it, although evidence showed he knew it was going to happen.

The sheriff, not present for any of the beatings, was found liable for damages of $125,000. This liability was based, in part, on the fact that supervisors knew of the beatings and did nothing to prevent them. The court felt the sheriff helped conceal the incidents by failing to investigate them. The failure to investigate also suggested to the court that the sheriff "ratified" the illegal beatings. *Marchese v. Lucas*, 758 F.2d 1816 (6th Cir., 1985).

Other supervisory failures potentially can lead to supervisory liability. These include such things as improper supervision or assignment, gross failures in hiring and retention (hiring and/or retaining clearly incompetent staff), failures in directing of staff, and so forth.

The common link in all of these areas is where the supervisor's alleged failure can be tied directly to the actual violation, and it can be said that but for the failure of the supervisor, this violation probably would not have occurred. In this sense, the courts will say that the supervisor "caused" the violation.

Failure-to-train lawsuits are not brought against the trainer or first-level supervisor. Instead, the agency or agency head is sued. The lawsuit claims that the inadequate training or supervision reflected agency policy or custom.

"Should Have Known" Liability

Several years ago, supervisory liability claims would be based on arguments that officials knew or should have known about a particular problem and failed to take proper remedial action. However, the Supreme Court rejected the idea that what an official "should have known" could be the basis for finding the official liable.[4] A pre-operative transsexual sued various federal prison officials for showing deliberate indifference to his safety needs by placing him in a men's federal penitentiary, where he claimed to have been sexually assaulted. The Court said that to be deliberately indifferent, an official must have actual knowledge of

25

an excessive risk to an inmate and then must disregard that risk. What the official arguably should have known cannot be the basis for liability.

Forms of Relief under the Civil Rights Act

Two basic forms of relief are available under the Civil Rights Act for the plaintiff who establishes that his or her rights have been violated—injunctions and damages.

Injunctions

Injunctions are orders from a court to a defendant that require the defendant to stop (or start) doing something. For example, "Stop denying inmates adequate medical care" or "To meet your obligations to provide adequate medical care, increase the number of medical professionals providing care to inmates." Injunctions are historically the most common form of relief under the Civil Rights Act and are what frequently led to the (generally inappropriate) complaint that courts are improperly meddling with state affairs. Injunctions under Section 1983 have led to the reshaping and reformatting of entire correctional systems.

Failure to comply with an injunction subjects the defendant to potential sanctions for contempt of court, including fines and even imprisonment. Failure to comply with injunctions worded in general terms also frequently has led to more specific injunctions. This is particularly true in conditions-of-confinement suits.

The Prison Litigation Reform Act (PLRA) attempts to reduce the power of the federal courts to enter injunctions in jail and prison cases. First, any injunction must be "narrowly drawn, extend no further than necessary to correct the violation of the Federal right, and [be] the least intrusive means necessary to correct the violation of the Federal right."[5]

The PLRA also forbids courts from issuing orders that have the effect of reducing or limiting a prison population, such as a population cap or release orders, until other less intrusive forms of relief have been attempted for a reasonable period of time and found inadequate.[6] Even then, only a three-judge court can enter a prisoner release order. As of late 2007, only one court has entered a PLRA population-reduction order. A motion for a population-reduction order is pending against the California Department of Corrections. If granted, it could affect tens of thousands of inmates. Within a few months of the PLRA's passage, the Supreme Court also discussed the power of lower courts to order injunctive relief against prison officials. In *Lewis v. Casey,*[7] the Court was quite critical of a very detailed relief order a district court entered in an access to the courts case (see Chapter 4 for a discussion of this aspect of the decision). *Lewis* emphasizes that when a lower court finds constitutional violations in a correctional facility, it should consider the view of prison officials in formulating a relief order and try to defer to the judgment of those officials. A court should try to avoid becoming too involved in overseeing day-to-day operational matters. The general tone of the *Lewis* decision is very similar to that of the PLRA, although interestingly, the *Lewis* opinion does not mention the PLRA.

Damages

Monetary damages are available under Section 1983. Damages are of the following three types:

1. **Nominal.** Where the plaintiff's rights were violated but the plaintiff can show no actual harm, the plaintiff is entitled only to "nominal" damages, usually $1.00.

2. **Compensatory.** These compensate the plaintiff for injuries actually suffered. They include such objective factors as lost wages and medical expenses. Compensatory damages also cover more subjective forms of loss such as pain and suffering and mental anguish.

   The Prison Litigation Reform Act (*see* Chapter 2) limits an inmate's ability to obtain compensatory damages by providing that no action can be brought for mental or emotional injury suffered while in custody without a prior showing of physical injury, 42 USC § 1997e(e).

3. **Punitive.** Punitive damages are intended to punish the wrongdoer and deter similar sorts of conduct by others in the future. They usually are awarded only when the defendant knowingly violated the Constitution and/or acted in reckless disregard of the rights of the plaintiff.

   Where the right allegedly violated was not "clearly established," the defendant will be granted a "qualified immunity" and cannot be required to pay damages. Sometimes this is known as the "good-faith" defense, although this is something of a misnomer. Whether an employee is entitled to qualified immunity in a particular situation typically focuses on the legal question of whether the law at issue was "clearly established" and not on whether the employee was acting in subjective good faith.

The qualified immunity defense is court-created and recognizes that government officials should not be held liable in damages for failing to predict accurately the future course of constitutional law. It protects only employees—it does not protect a government agency if that agency, such as a city or county, is otherwise subject to damages. The qualified-immunity defense only protects against damages, not against injunctive relief.

Despite the implications of the name, "good-faith defense," an employee's subjective good intentions or good faith are of little relevance in establishing a qualified-immunity defense. Rather than focusing on the employee's state of mind, the good-faith defense focuses almost entirely on the state of the law at the time of the incident: the key question is whether the law was "clearly established."

Employees of private corrections companies do not have any qualified immunity protection. In 1997, the Supreme Court said that the policy reasons that underlay protecting governmental employees from liability damages unless a constitutional right was clearly established do not extend to employees of private companies, even though they are doing the same work as correctional officials employed by government agencies.[8]

In some situations, even broader immunity is available, as in the case where a probation officer is acting so closely with a sentencing judge that a court will afford the probation officer complete judicial or quasi-judicial immunity. Judicial or quasi-judicial immunity affords the person protected by it almost complete immunity from damage lawsuits. In general, only qualified (not quasi-judicial) immunity is available for most correctional employees.

In 1986, the Supreme Court decided if hearing officers in prison disciplinary hearings were entitled to quasi-judicial immunity. These officials make a great many constitutionally important decisions, and they decide disciplinary cases, which is somewhat comparable to what judges do. However, the Court refused to extend complete immunity to these officials, at least as long as they are still direct subordinates of the warden and are subject to pressure from other correctional staff to decide cases in favor of the institution.[9]

As correctional law continues to evolve and develop, an increasing number of rights are becoming "clearly established." Therefore, potential liability damage is increasing.

Attorneys' Fees

Under another part of the U.S. Code, 42 USC 1988, the prevailing party in a civil rights action is entitled to attorneys' fees. The Attorneys' Fees Act primarily benefits prevailing plaintiffs since the law has been interpreted to allow fees for prevailing defendants only when the plaintiff's action can be shown to have been frivolous (a difficult burden to meet).

Prior to passage of the Prison Litigation Reform Act, courts generally interpreted the Attorneys' Fee Act liberally under the theory that by encouraging civil rights litigation, more civil rights violations would be brought to the attention of the courts and corrected, thus furthering the underlying purposes of the Civil Rights Act. The general method of computing fees was to multiply the hours the lawyer spent on the case times the lawyer's hourly billing rate. This produced a so-called "lodestar" figure, which might be adjusted up or down slightly. Fee awards based on hourly rates sometimes more than $300 per hour were not uncommon. Courts sometimes gave fee awards worth many times more than the judgment, which the plaintiff won. Very large, complex cases could generate fees in the millions of dollars.

The PLRA changed this. The law now limits the hourly rate for attorney's fee awards in inmate cases to150 percent of the hourly rate paid to appointed criminal defense lawyers. This limits fees to less than $150/hour in most jurisdictions. Fees must also bear a reasonable relationship to the size of the judgment awarded the plaintiff. These and other restrictions have reduced the size of attorneys' fee awards considerably. However, even with these limitations, attorneys' fees will remain an important part of inmate civil rights litigation.

While it sounds like the possibility of obtaining a fee award in excess of $200 per hour would have attracted many lawyers in private practice to the field of correctional law, this does not appear to have been the case. To the extent that lawyers were attracted by the possibility of obtaining such fees (after perhaps years of litigating a case without receiving any money), reducing the possible fee award to $150 per hour or less is likely to discourage private lawyers from representing inmates.

The limitation on attorney's fees that the PLRA imposes applies only to actions brought by prisoners. If a former inmate brings the suit, the limitation generally would not apply; nor would it apply if the estate of a deceased inmate brings the suit. Thus, the limitation does not apply to some significant types of suits that involve "inmate rights."

CRIPA and the Justice Department

Legislation permits another significant type of inmate suit. As part of the Civil Right of Institutionalized Persons Act (CRIPA), Congress authorized the U.S. Department of Justice to bring civil right lawsuits on behalf of persons in all types of institutions, including prisons and jails.

The CRIPA process begins with a thorough investigation of an institution by experts retained by the Justice Department. The investigation leads to a formal written report that may describe problems found by the experts that the Justice Department deems of constitutional significance and outlines the remedial steps the Department of Justice believes necessary. The agency under investigation can then negotiate a settlement without a lawsuit being filed or reject any possibility of settlement In the latter situation, the Department of Justice is likely to file a §1983 action against the agency.

In 2007, investigation letters were issued regarding jails or prisons in Washington State, Tennessee, and Hawaii. In 2008-2009, the Justice Department conducted more than 100 investigations of prisons and jails.[10] While not all these have led to litigation, a number of settlements and have resulted from such investigations.

Grievances

Under the Civil Rights of Institutionalized Persons Act (CRIPA), a federal court could postpone action on an inmate civil rights case until the inmates exhausted their remedies under a grievance system if the system met certain standards and either the U.S. Department of Justice or the federal court approved it. Relatively few jurisdictions took advantage of this law, probably because of objections to the content of the standards, which a grievance system had to meet to be certified.

The PLRA expands the exhaustion requirement. Now, an inmate must exhaust any available grievance or appeal mechanism, not just one that meets federal standards. This means that if inmates do not file a grievance about a matter, they probably will not be able to file later a civil rights case about the same matter.

The Supreme Court has strictly interpreted the exhaustion requirement. This means that the inmates must exhaust an administrative remedy—even if it cannot provide the remedy the inmate seeks, such as damages.[11] Inmates must completely exhaust available remedies. Thus, if inmates miss a deadline for taking a step under the agency's grievance process, agency rules bar them from continuing the process, and the inmates fail to exhaust their remedies. If this occurs, the courts cannot consider their civil rights complaint.[12] Depending on the language of an agency's grievance process, the failure of inmates to file a grievance within a few days of the incident can bar the inmates from having their grievance considered. In turn, this prevents them from pursuing a civil rights case, despite any merit their claim might have.

Torts

A tort is a civil (as opposed to criminal) wrong and arises when there is a violation of some duty that the defendant owes the plaintiff. A classic type of tort case is the suit that arises from the negligent operation of an automobile, in which the negligence of the defendant (the failure to use reasonable care) injures the plaintiff. The "duty" of the operator of the car is to show reasonable care in operating the automobile, so as not to endanger another person.

State statute sometimes defines what "reasonable care" is in a given situation, but more often, the courts define it through the common law. The common law comes from the courts as they define and apply principles of custom and historic usage (as opposed to principles from laws passed by legislative bodies). The common law traces back to the fundamental principles and rules of action defined by the English courts.

Tort actions common in corrections include such issues as the negligent loss of property, failure to protect the inmate from harm, medical malpractice, or breaches of other duties of reasonable care that correctional staff may owe inmates or others. Improper training, supervision, or assignment of staff also can be the basis of a negligence claim against a supervisor. In some states, victims of crimes committed by persons under some form of supervision (probation, parole, and so forth) are able to sue supervising officials and agencies under theories of negligent release or supervision.

A tort suit seeks only damages. Typically, inmates or their lawyers file tort suits in state court.

Often, a lawsuit about a particular subject, such as medical care, may be brought as either a tort or a civil rights claim. The legal burden the plaintiff may have to meet to win is often different between a tort and a civil rights claim, even when the operative facts in the case are the same. For example, if an inmate feels he or she has received inadequate medical care, the claim in a tort suit would be one of negligence. Yet, if a person brings a civil rights claim, the claim would have to demonstrate "deliberate indifference to serious medical needs," a more difficult burden than showing simple negligence.

Inmates often prefer to file civil rights suits, even when the burden in those cases may be greater than in tort suits. There are several reasons for this.

1. Historically, people view federal courts (where civil rights cases usually are brought) as more sympathetic to inmate claims than are state courts, the site of a tort suit.

2. The scope of possible relief in a civil rights case may be broader than in a tort. No injunctive relief is available in a tort. State law sometimes limits the amount of damages that can be awarded against government officials or may immunize those officials from damages altogether. Some states do not allow punitive damages. These limitations do not apply in civil rights cases.

3. Attorneys' fee awards, available in civil rights cases, are not available in tort suits.

Habeas Corpus

In a habeas corpus action, petitioners claim that they are being held in custody illegally in violation of some constitutional right. A habeas corpus petition typically will not relate to anything a correctional employee did or did not do. Instead, it will attack an action of the court or agency responsible for the individual being in custody. Habeas corpus petitions name the custodian of the person as the respondent (defendant). Therefore, the name of the warden of a prison frequently will appear on the pleadings.

Sometimes an inmate will challenge the results of a disciplinary hearing in a habeas corpus proceeding, in which case an individual employee could be involved directly with the case. Most states allow inmates to file some form of a habeas corpus petition in state court. When inmates can show they have "exhausted state remedies," they can file a habeas corpus petition in federal court. While habeas corpus petitions become a form of appeal beyond normal appeal proceedings, they are limited to constitutional issues.

Through habeas corpus petitions, persons under sentence of death may repeatedly challenge their death sentence. The only relief obtainable in a habeas corpus proceeding is release from custody.

The number of habeas corpus petitions filed by state inmates in 2008 was 18,450.[13] This is about double what it was in 1988.

Other Types of Lawsuits

A correctional officer may see other types of suits. An officer may be involved directly in personnel actions that can end up in court. Officers themselves may bring claims relating to discrimination based on race, sex, disability, or other reason (*see* Chapters 12 and 13). Passage of the Americans with Disabilities Act (ADA) (*see* Chapter 14) has resulted in many more claims brought by both officers and inmates concerning treatment of disabilities.

Lawsuits over civil rights are typically "civil" actions, seeking injunctive relief or damages. However, the U.S. Department of Justice also has the authority to charge individual correctional officers and officials with criminal violations of inmates' civil rights.

Conclusion

While very few actions filed by or on behalf of inmates against correctional personnel result in a judgment in favor of the plaintiff, civil rights actions and federal habeas corpus petitions have had a tremendous effect on the administration of corrections in America since the late 1960s. Entire correctional systems have been reformed as a result of civil rights actions. Institutional disciplinary processes take the form they do because of civil rights suits. Due process in parole and probation revocation proceedings is required because of the courts interpreting and applying constitutional principles. Many other examples support the theory that civil rights actions probably have been the single greatest agent for change in corrections in this century.

The expansion of inmate rights has slowed—some would say it has even reversed itself to some degree—in recent years. The biggest factor in this change has been the increasingly conservative Supreme Court, which in decision after decision has chipped away at inmates' rights. Passage of the Prison Litigation Reform Act, while not changing any substantive rights of inmates, discourages inmates from filing as many lawsuits as they had been filing. As the federal courts become less receptive to inmate complaints, inmate litigation may shift from the federal courts to the state courts as the inmate seeks relief under various provisions of state constitutions.

Review Questions

1. List three types of lawsuits most commonly filed by inmates.

2. True or False: A state cannot be sued directly in a civil rights action.

3. Give one example of when a supervisor could be held liable in a civil rights action, even if the supervisor did not take part directly in the actions that led to the suit.

Endnotes

1. *Monell v. Department of Social Services*, 98 S.Ct. 2018 (1978).

2. *West v. Atkins*, 487 U.S. 42 (1988).

3. *Kahle v. Leonard*, 477 F.3d 344 (8th Cir., 2007).

4. *City of Canton v. Harris*, 489 U.S. 378 (1989).

5. *Farmer v. Brennan*, 511 U.S. 824 (1994).

6. 18 USC § 3626(a).

7. *Lewis v. Casey*, 518 U.S. 343 (1996).

8. *Richardson v. McKnight*, 521 U.S. 399 (1997).

9. *Cleavinger v. Saxner*, 106 S.Ct. 496 (1986).

10. http://www.justice.gov/crt/split/jails.php accessed. April 29, 2010.

11. *Booth v. Churner*, 532 U.S. 731 (2001).

12. *Woodford v. Ngo*, 126 S.Ct. 2378 (2006)

13. *Sourcebook of Criminal Justice Statistics*, 2008, Table 5.65. Department of Justice, Bureau of Justice Statistics. *Sourcebook of Criminal Justice Statistics Online*. 2009. http://www.albany.edu/sourcebook/pdf/t5652008.pdf

Chapter 4:
Access to the Courts

The idea of anyone—inmate or free person—having rights of any kind becomes meaningless if there is no way the person can have these rights enforced. In any society, rules (which often translate into "rights") must govern the conduct and relations between people and organizations (including government). Conflicts develop over whether people have followed these rules in a given situation. These disputes might range from an argument between two neighbors about where the boundary line between their properties lies, to arguments between a state and the federal government over whether a federal law unconstitutionally infringes on the state's sovereignty in some way. These disputes include questions of the relationship between inmates and the government agencies and employees who keep them in custody.[1]

Some process is necessary to resolve these disputes, to decide if one person has violated someone's rights and if so, to then decide what should be done to remedy the situation. In America, our local, state, and federal court systems exist for this purpose. Without the courts or some similar dispute-resolving body with the power to enforce its decisions, rights would belong only to the strongest, and any freedoms "guaranteed" by laws or the Constitution would become hollow and often only illusory.

The primary function of the courts is to determine if someone's rights (constitutional rights, statutory rights, and so forth) have been violated. If they have, the courts determine what sort of remedy is appropriate. Because these duties may require judging the actions of government agencies and interpreting and evaluating laws, the courts exist as a separate branch of government, independent of the legislative and executive branches.

Inmates' Access to the Courts

However, having a court system to protect rights and resolve disputes will have no meaning if a person cannot get a dispute into court. So, while the Constitution nowhere contains the phrase "access to the courts," the Supreme Court has long held that the right of access to the courts is inherently part of the concept of due process, if not other parts of the Constitution, as well.

Not only is there a constitutionally protected right of access to the courts, but that right is very important and fundamental, since all other rights may depend on a person being able to get to court. For persons not in custody, the right of access to the courts is seldom an issue. If individuals feel their rights have been violated, they can hire a lawyer and file a suit. Alternatively, if they cannot afford a lawyer, they can research the law, prepare the suit themselves, and file it with the appropriate court.

The right of access to the courts is much more of an issue for persons in custody than it is for those not in prison or jail because the institution literally can be a physical barrier between the inmate and lawyers, legal research materials, and the courts. The Supreme Court first began to recognize a right of access to the courts for inmates in 1941 in the *Hull* case: ". . . the state and its officers may not abridge or impair [an inmate's] right to apply to a federal court for a writ of habeas corpus."[2]

This case arose because the State of Michigan had a policy that required any suit that an inmate wanted to file had to be approved by the lawyer for the state parole board, to be sure the suit was "in proper form." The Court said it was unconstitutional for the state to set up this sort of barrier between the inmate and the court.

A number of years later, a Tennessee policy prohibiting one inmate from helping another with a suit was challenged. The Supreme Court held in *Johnson v. Avery* that the prison may impose certain reasonable *limitations* and regulations on one inmate assisting another, but cannot prohibit such activity, at least until the prison provides reasonable alternative forms of assistance to the inmates.[3] "Writ-writers," or "jailhouse lawyers," inmates who help other inmates with suits, remain a fixture in correctional institutions.

The next time the Supreme Court looked at an access to the courts question was in 1974 in a case more famous for its holdings about inmate disciplinary hearings, *Wolff v. McDonnell.*[4] Buried in the last pages of the opinion is a discussion of the question of whether inmates' right of access to the courts pertained only to filing habeas corpus petitions (both the Hull and Avery cases involved just habeas corpus petitions) or whether the right included civil rights cases brought under 42 USC § 1983. The court held that the right included civil rights cases.

The fourth and by far the most important Supreme Court access-to-the-courts case came in 1977 with *Bounds v. Smith*, when the Court went beyond saying the state could not impose barriers between inmates and the courts and instead said the state had an affirmative duty to assist inmates:

> . . . the fundamental constitutional right of access to the courts requires prison authorities to assist inmates in the preparation and filing of meaningful legal papers by providing prisoners with adequate law libraries or adequate assistance from persons trained in the law.[5]

The *Bounds* case involved a challenge to the resources the North Carolina Department of Corrections provided its inmates, who were scattered throughout the state in more than seventy different institutions, many of which were quite small.

By the time the case reached the Supreme Court, North Carolina had agreed to provide major libraries in several central locations and to move inmates to those libraries on request. The Supreme Court approved this plan and the contents of the libraries that North Carolina proposed.[6]

While *Bounds* talked about adequate law libraries or access to persons trained in the law, most institutions opted to provide law libraries rather than lawyers or other legally trained assistance. Some systems, for example, Florida, provided large law libraries staffed with trained inmate law clerks. *Bounds*, therefore, became known as the "law library" case.

After *Bounds*, access to the courts cases usually fall into one of two categories:

1. Cases that claim an individual officer did something to prevent an inmate from pursuing a legal claim such as destroying the inmate's legal papers.

2. Cases that dealt with the adequacy of the system an institution provided to assist inmates in pursuing legal claims. These cases would typically look at the contents of the law library, the size of the library, its hours of operation, and whether inmates could get enough time in the library to prepare their legal papers.

Case Study: Legal Materials Lost

Texas inmate, Jabri McCullough, worked for seven years on his legal research, reviewing legal correspondence and poring over his trial transcripts looking for errors that might lead to a reversal of his criminal conviction. One day, officers confiscated all his legal materials on the basis that he had excess property in his cell and the material was improperly stored. The defendants later conceded that Mr. McCullough did not have excess property.

Under agency rules, the inmate was supposed to receive and sign a formal notice about confiscated property that, among other things, explained how he could get the property back. Mr. McCullough never got that notice.

Mr. McCullough tried more than a dozen times, orally and in writing, to get the property back, all to no avail. Eventually, the property was destroyed even though under Department rules Mr. McCullough had a right to have the material returned. One official was primarily responsible for approving the confiscation, failing to provide the proper notice to the inmate, and ordering the destruction of the material.

The court found these actions violated Mr. McCullough's right of access to the courts and ordered the official mentioned above to pay Mr. McCullough $22,400 in compensatory damages. To emphasize the message the court was sending, the judge tacked on another $22,400 in punitive damages and ordered the official to replace as much of the material (such as trial transcripts) as possible. *McCullough v. Johnson*, 2007 WL 3406753 (N.D. Tex., 2007).

The duty to provide "meaningful assistance" extends to jails, not just prisons, although what is required in jails may be slightly different in light of the relatively short time most inmates spend in jail. However, for inmates in jail for periods of several months or more, the right probably is virtually identical.

In 1996, the Supreme Court revisited the area of access to the courts for the first time since its 1977 decision in *Bounds* in *Lewis v. Casey*.[7] In this case, which involved the access to the courts system in the Arizona Department of Corrections, the Court generally reaffirmed the principle in *Bounds* that institutions have the affirmative duty to provide inmates with assistance in the form of law libraries or persons trained in the law. However, the Court also made it much more difficult for inmates to sue successfully about denial of their right of access to the courts by saying that to win such a claim, the inmates must prove they had been harmed ("prejudiced") in some way as a result of inadequate legal resources. An example of such harm would be if the inmate had a suit actually dismissed because of the inadequate resources available.

Tourscher v. McCullough[8] is typical of many inmate-access-to-the-courts cases after *Lewis*. The inmate complained that Pennsylvania prison officials violated his right of access to the courts by making him work in the prison cafeteria while his conviction was on appeal. Both the district court and court of appeals dismissed this argument. The court of appeals noted that Mr. Tourscher had failed to make any sort of a showing that his cafeteria work interfered with his ability to prosecute his appeal in state court. Absent a showing of this sort of injury, his case failed to state a claim.

Law Libraries and Lewis v. Casey—A Right Redefined

Under *Bounds*, and before *Lewis*, a very common access to the courts claim related to the adequacy of prison law libraries. Remember, *Bounds* had said one way prison officials could comply with their duty to provide some level of assistance to inmates was through law libraries. Most prisons and jails chose to try to meet their *Bounds* obligations through providing law libraries in some form, instead of providing "assistance from persons trained in the law," another alternative mentioned in *Bounds*.

Courts commonly required agencies to buy very substantial law libraries, costing tens of thousands of dollars to purchase and thousands every year to maintain. Along with lawsuits about what should be in the library were claims about such things as how much access time had to be provided, the adequacy of the space where the books were kept, and how access could be provided to inmates in segregated units, who could not physically come to the library.[9] A number of law libraries considered adequate under standards the courts used before *Lewis* might be available in major prisons or large jails, but typically were not available in smaller facilities.

As institutions increased their reliance on books, questions began to arise around how the most complete law library could provide adequate access to the courts for the inmate who could not read. Since many prison inmates are illiterate, or have very limited reading skills, this became a serious question. The author of this book served as an expert witness in one case in which the prison system was investing substantial amounts of time and effort to provide trained inmate law clerks who, it was felt, could provide assistance to illiterate inmates.

The affirmative duties for correctional administrators that began in *Bounds* seemed to keep growing. This growth perhaps reached its zenith in *Lewis*, and in doing so, proved to be the straw that may have broken the camel's back. The district court in *Lewis* found that the access to the courts system that the Arizona Department of Corrections provided its inmates was not sufficient. Inadequacies related to such things as the training of library staff, updating legal materials, and photocopying. Inmates segregated from the main prison population and illiterate or non-English speaking inmates were specially affected by the inadequacies. Most of the court's negative conclusions were not based on evidence that inmates had been harmed, but rather on the idea that inmates at some point might be harmed in pursuing a legal claim.

Although the trial only showed two inmates who actually had been injured by inadequacies in the Arizona system, the court ordered systemwide relief. The court appointed a special master to assist the court in formulating a plan for relief. After eight months, he produced what became, with minor changes, a court-ordered blueprint for the operation of the access-to-the-courts system. The plan went into minute detail, including the number of hours law libraries were to be kept open, the content of a video course for training inmate law clerks, and the educational requirements for prison librarians.

When *Lewis* reached the Supreme Court, a majority of the Court did not welcome the result with open arms. The Court reversed the lower court decision. In doing so, the Court changed the way courts must analyze access-to-the-courts claims, encouraged innovations other than the traditional law library, and was extremely critical of the lower court's detailed order. At one point, the opinion notes ". . . the injunction imposed by the District Court was inordinately—indeed wildly—intrusive."[10] *Lewis* then becomes an important case both for access-to-the-courts issues and for questions regarding court injunctive orders in reform cases.

The "actual injury" requirement from *Lewis* makes it harder for inmates to win access-to-the-courts claims. It is now common to see access-to-the-courts cases dismissed because the inmate failed to show he or she suffered harm or prejudice caused by the institution's law library or other access-to-the-courts program. Inmates cannot allege, in conclusory fashion, that the lack of resources prejudiced their attempt to pursue a legal claim.

"To avoid [dismissal of the case], a prisoner must make specific allegations as to the prejudice suffered because of the defendants' alleged conduct. . . such as by alleging that he missed court deadlines, failed to make timely filings, or that legitimate claims were dismissed because of the denial of reasonable access to legal resources." *Lewis* also puts other limits on the right of access to the courts. The case makes it clear that the right of access to the courts protects the inmates' ability to challenge their criminal conviction or prison conditions and practices. It does not protect the inmates' ability to seek judicial relief for other matters, such as pursuing parenting or child custody claims, which may be important to some inmates.

"In other words, [the right of access to the courts] does not guarantee inmates the wherewithal to transform themselves into litigating engines capable of filing everything from shareholder derivative actions to slip-and-fall claims."[11] In saying this, the Supreme Court did not mean that inmates are barred from filing such claims, only that the prison has no constitutional duty to help them do so.

Lewis adds another important limit on the duty of prisons and jails under *Bounds*. The affirmative duty to provide assistance in some form only allows the inmates to bring a grievance to court, not necessarily to discover if they have a grievance or to litigate effectively once a case gets to court.

The problem of dealing with the illiterate inmate remains after *Lewis*. The opinion notes the problem, but does not address it in any way. However, it remains obvious that any access to the courts system that relies on an inmate's ability to read, whether it be legal forms, or sophisticated legal treatises, cannot help the inmate who cannot read. Sooner or later, such an inmate will have a nonfrivolous legal claim of the sort protected by *Lewis* and will not be able to bring that claim if he or she cannot find some form of assistance. What form that assistance must take remains to be decided in future lawsuits.

Perhaps the most significant aspect of *Lewis* is one that is slow to develop. The opinion clearly states that *Bounds*, as interpreted by *Lewis*, does not create an inmate's right to a law library. The Court encourages agencies to experiment with other means of providing assistance, suggesting that a combination of minimal access to legal advice and to legal forms might be enough. At least some agencies have moved to replace their law libraries with this type of program, but there is not yet a body of lower court decisions that analyze this approach.

Perhaps the most dramatic example of the impact of *Lewis* comes from Arizona, where the case originally arose. After winning in the Supreme Court, the Arizona Department of Corrections replaced its law libraries with a limited number of contract paralegals charged with providing very limited forms of legal assistance to inmates. They cannot file lawsuits for the inmates, prepare legal pleadings, or give inmates specific legal advice about a potential claim. As bare bones as this system is, no inmate has successfully challenged it in court.

Questions about law libraries have long been the subject of extensive litigation. For many years, the meaning of the right of access to the courts seemed to be constantly expanding. *Lewis* put the brakes on this expansion. The case allows agencies to reexamine how they provide inmates with legal assistance and forces courts to take a different, more conservative approach in defining the details of the right of access to the courts.

Dealing with the Litigious Inmate

Some inmates seem to make a career out of filing lawsuits. One Washington State inmate filed more than 200 lawsuits in a five-year period.[12] Every state has a similar example. Courts have concluded that at least some of these litigious inmates file suits primarily as a means of harassing and vexing both the court and the correctional employees named as defendants.[13]

Why can't something be done about this abuse of the legal process? Why don't the courts just dismiss cases without requiring the government to invest the time and money necessary to respond? Why can't institutions take action against inmates for filing suits that have no merit by disciplining them or denying them privileges?

Over the years, some courts have tried to impose some limitations on litigious inmates. These have included requiring inmates with some funds to pay at least part of the filing fees normally charged a person wishing to file a lawsuit in federal district court (the filing fee is now $350). In cases of extreme abuse, courts may try to limit the number of suits the inmate can file or set other extraordinary requirements for an inmate to proceed with a suit. However, these efforts have been sporadic and have had little or no impact on the steady increase of inmate suits prior to passage of the Prison Litigation Reform Act. Inmate civil rights filings generally increased at about the same rate at which the total inmate population has increased between 1970 and 1995.

The Prison Litigation Reform Act (PLRA) attacks the "frequent filer" problem in a couple of ways. The requirement that inmates pay filing fees on the time-payment plan (as opposed to waiving fees altogether) combined with other changes made by the PLRA has dramatically reduced the number of suits inmates file. The filing fee changes now require institution officials to withdraw funds from the inmate's account and send them to the court to pay a filing-fee debt. The system does not depend on the inmate choosing to send money.

The three-strikes provision of the PLRA hinders the frequent filer even more directly by barring inmates from filing future cases after three cases have been dismissed as frivolous, malicious, or failing to state a claim. Many inmate cases are dismissed on the latter ground, so the inmates who file one case after another are likely to work themselves quickly into three-strike status. The exception to the three-strikes rule, where there is a showing the inmate is in "imminent danger of serious physical injury" should not prove to be a major loophole in the three-strikes provision.

The three-strikes' inmate can avoid this bar by paying the full court filing fee when he or she files the complaint. However, few inmates have $350 at one time or are willing to spend it on filing a lawsuit.

One of the major goals of Congress in passing the PRLA was to reduce the number of lawsuits inmates filed. In this respect, the law has succeeded, probably as a combination of the filing fee and the three-strikes' requirements. The number of civil rights lawsuits inmates filed grew every year from 1970 until 1996, with one minor exception. In 1995, inmates filed slightly more than 39,000 such cases in federal district court. By 2001, five years after passage of the PLRA, that number had dropped to 22,200, a decrease of about 43 percent. The decrease in the rate at which inmates file cases is even more dramatic. In 1995, there were nearly 25 civil rights cases filed per 1,000 inmates. By 2001, the number had dropped to just over 1/1,000 inmates. By 2005, the number of filings began to increase slowly, passing 24,300 in 2008.[14]

Retaliation

Staff members have a natural tendency to want to "get back" at an inmate who files a lawsuit against the staff member that seeks millions of dollars in damages, especially when the staff member may realize the suit has little or no merit. Regardless of the merits (or lack thereof) of the original suit, retaliation against an inmate for filing a lawsuit violates the inmate's right of access to the courts. Doing so would punish individuals for exercising their constitutional rights. Just as the institution may not set up barriers between inmates and the courts before they file lawsuits, neither the institution nor staff may impose official or unofficial penalties on inmates because they filed a lawsuit.

Case Study: Do Not Threaten Federal Judges

Robert Dixon, a Georgia inmate trying to sue various county officials made a serious tactical error in pursuing his case. Apparently frustrated by court orders on procedural matters that he felt were slowing the progress of his case, Mr. Dixon fired off a letter to the court that said "If you don't stop trying to dismiss my case for no reason . . . I will have my boys in Atlanta kill you and your family. I am from the ATL [sic] and can get you dead with one phone call." Mr. Dixon actually sent the letter to the wrong court but it eventually found its way to the judge presiding over his case.

The case, which involved various conditions of confinement Mr. Dixon faced while in the county jail, came before the court on defendants' motion for summary judgment. The judge granted the motion on the merits and was ready to dismiss the case when he paused to discuss the threatening letter. Needless to say, the judge was very displeased with the document.

"Plaintiff cannot clamor for justice while using the same breath to threaten the trial judge. Consequently, the Court also determines that it is appropriate to grant Defendants' motion for summary judgment as a sanction for Plaintiff's conduct, irrespective of the merits of the case." *Dixon v. Toole*, 2006 WL 1938433 (S.D. Ga., 2006).

The outspoken inmate may also face criminal charges for his intemperate remarks. You do not threaten federal judges.

Attorney's Visits

Courts unanimously have recognized the right of a lawyer to visit a client in prison. This also includes the right of persons working for a lawyer, such as investigators or law clerks, to visit inmate clients of the lawyer.

While the institution can impose reasonable regulations on when lawyers may visit, the key word is "reasonable." Any such limitations should be flexible and recognize the legitimate need for access outside of normal working hours (when the lawyer may be in trial). Communication between the lawyer and the client is privileged, and institution staff may not eavesdrop on such conversation

Indigence

Where an inmate is indigent, the institution must provide reasonable amounts of postage and supplies (paper, pens, and so forth) for the inmate wishing to exercise the right of access to the courts.[15] A problem may arise in defining indigence for purposes of deciding when an inmate is entitled to stamps. Again, rules in this area need to be flexible. Most courts have said inmates do not have a right of access to copy machines.[16]

Case Study: Inmates Can Wear Out Their Welcome to the Courts

Inmate Debro Siddig Abdul-Akbar filed suit complaining about various alleged problems of obtaining access to the courts. Rather than having the court smooth out these problems, he found the court actually put up barriers to his filing more lawsuits.

The inmate had filed more than forty civil suits in a seven-year period. In response to the latest one, the district court dismissed the case as frivolous and ordered the court clerk to refuse to file any more cases for Abdul-Akbar unless he met certain extraordinary requirements. The court of appeals agreed such restrictions were appropriate in cases where there was a history of an inmate abusing the privilege of bringing a lawsuit *in forma pauperis*.[17]

But having said that Abdul-Akbar's history of abusing the *in forma pauperis* privilege justified such an injunction, the court reversed the lower court's dismissal of his latest lawsuit, saying the allegations in the complaint, if true, might state a claim for relief. *Abdul-Akbar v. Watson*, 901 F.2d 329 (3rd Cir., 1990).

Note that this case was decided before the Prison Litigation Reform Act was passed. Out of the forty cases the court mentioned, at least three were dismissed as frivolous, malicious, or for failing to state a claim. As a result, Mr. Akbar now would have to pay the full $350 filing fee to get almost any suit he might attempt to file accepted by the court.

Appointed Counsel

A variety of issues arise from time to time under the general duty of providing inmates with "meaningful" access to the courts. What about appointed counsel? Many jail inmates are represented by lawyers in their pending criminal cases. Do these lawyers, often paid for by the state, provide adequate access to the courts? They probably do not.

The fact that jail inmates have a lawyer appointed in their criminal case will not assure that the inmate is being provided "meaningful access to the courts" under *Bounds*, because often the appointed counsel will not be able to provide the inmate with any advice or assistance outside of the criminal case. Even where appointed counsel arguably do provide meaningful access to the courts for their clients, this still leaves the jail with the need to provide resources for the sentenced inmates housed in the jail, who no longer are represented by counsel.

Conclusion

The right of access to the courts has proven controversial in practice. In theory, it is hard to argue against the concept that individuals should be able to file a lawsuit, which claims their rights under the Constitution have been violated. While some very important decisions in corrections began with one inmate filing a lawsuit by himself or herself, the tens of thousands of inmate claims dismissed by federal courts every year without even a trial, perhaps without even a response from defendants, shows how little merit most inmate suits have.

Courts have been very reluctant to take steps that might check the flow of inmate lawsuits. Congress, in passing the Prison Litigation Reform Act, has stepped in where courts have not in an attempt to cut down on the number of inmate civil rights claims. As of 2009, the total number of inmate civil rights claims filed in federal court has decreased sharply. While undoubtedly this change prevents many cases with no merit from being filed, it also undoubtedly prevents many cases that have merit from ever being filed.

Review Questions

1. Why is the right of access to the courts an important part of America's legal system?

2. If an inmate is represented by appointed counsel in a criminal case, why is this not necessarily sufficient access to the courts?

3. What is the major vulnerability of an access-to-the-courts system, which is built around books and other written materials?

Endnotes

1. Schlanger, Margo. Inmate Litigation 116, *Harvard Law Review* 1157 (2003). This 150- page article is a fascinating discussion of the right of access to the courts and is laden with data about inmate litigation.

2. *Ex Parte Hull*, 312 U.S. 546 (1941).

3. *Johnson v. Avery*, 393 U.S. 483 (1969).

4. *Wolff v. McDonnell*, 418 U.S. 539 (1974), see Chapter 6.

5. *Bounds v. Smith*, 430 U.S. 817 (1977).

6. *Smith v. Bounds*, 813 F.2d 1299 (1979).

7. *Lewis v. Casey*, 116 S. Ct. 2174 (1996).

8. *Tourscher v. McCollough*, 184 F.3d 236 (3rd Cir., 1999).

9. *Touissaint v. McCarthy*, 597 F.Supp. 1388 (C.D. Cal., 1985).

10. 116 S.Ct. at 2185.

11. 116 S. Ct. at 2182.

12. *Demos v. Kincheloe*, E.D., Wash., #C-80-152-84 (unpublished).

13. *Doe v. State*, E.D. Wash., #C-83-409-JLQ, 1984 (unpublished).

14. www/Albany.edu/sourcebook/pdf/t5662008.pdf

15. PLRA 805, 28 USC Section 1915 A.

16. *Gittens v. Sullivan*, 848 F.2d 389 (2nd Cir. 1998).

17. *In forma pauperis* literally means "in the form or manner of a pauper." When any plaintiff (inmate or not) can establish that he or she is indigent and (at least in federal court) the suit does not appear to be frivolous or malicious, the normal filing fees are waived. Most inmates are granted *In forma pauperis* status.

Chapter 5:
Inmate Rights versus Institutional Interests: The Balancing Test

Many legal battles between inmates and jails or prisons center on a conflict between the right the inmate is claiming and a competing interest of the institution.

- An inmate wants to be able to wear a special religious medallion that, outside the institutional setting, would be of no concern to anyone, but prison officials are concerned that the medallion could be used as a weapon.

- Another inmate wants to receive a publication on martial arts techniques. Outside the facility, the publication might sell on a street corner newsstand. However, prison officials are concerned about inmates teaching themselves martial arts and using what they learn either against each other or against officers.

- A male inmate whose religious and personal beliefs require a great deal of modesty wants to avoid being seen in the nude by strangers, including staff. He is particularly offended at the thought of being seen by women while using the toilet. Yet, the institution requires inmates to be strip searched in certain circumstances and is using an increasing number of female officers as part of an equal opportunity program.

All of these conflicts—and many others—may wind up in court. The court will be asked to decide whether the inmates' constitutionally protected interests in exercising their freedom of religion, freedom of the press, the right to be free from unreasonable searches (or right to privacy) are outweighed by the concerns expressed by the institution.

Despite the absolute language of much of the Bill of Rights (such as part of the First Amendment: "Congress shall make no law respecting the establishment of religion, or prohibiting the free exercise thereof . . ."), it is clear that constitutional rights are not absolute. The government can limit the exercise of rights in certain situations. The dimensions of a particular right (such as the protection from unreasonable searches) vary from one situation to another. However, where constitutional rights—fundamental rights of all persons in this country—are restricted, the government must show a strong need to impose restrictions.

The challenge for the courts is to resolve disputes between persons desiring to exercise their rights in some way and the government's occasional desire to restrict that exercise. The court resolving such conflicts must balance the competing interests—the right versus the government's justification for its restriction—and decide which is the stronger. When is the government's concern strong enough to justify restricting someone from exercising a right guaranteed by the Constitution?

This sort of balancing approach has been a part of prisoners' rights litigation from its beginnings in the late 1960s. Surprisingly, the Supreme Court had rarely addressed how inmate rights should be weighed against institutional interests until the late 1980s. Then, in a series of cases decided between 1987 and early 1990, the Court addressed the question and developed a fundamental approach for analyzing the inmate right versus institutional-interest conflicts. This test applies to all such questions, regardless of what particular constitutional right is involved.

Prior to this series of cases, lower courts were busy developing their own balancing tests. Unfortunately, different courts developed different tests, some of which strongly favored the constitutional right and required a very strong, clear showing of need by the institution to justify any restriction of the right. Other courts went in the opposite direction, adopting tests that favored the institutional interests.

The result of this lower court activity was confusion and uncertainty. Depending on what legal test was applied to a given set of facts (such as a rule requiring short hair and no beards), one court might approve the rule while another would find it an unconstitutional infringement on the inmate's religious rights guaranteed by the First Amendment.

The uncertainty began to be clarified in 1987 with two decisions by the Supreme Court.[1] The facts of one clearly demonstrate the rule the Court adopted and how that rule is to be applied. These decisions, from more than two decades ago, continue to be the basis for analyzing and deciding many inmate lawsuits.

O'Lone v. Estate of Shabazz

In *O'Lone v. Estate of Shabazz*, a number of Muslim inmates at a medium-security prison in New Jersey challenged a rule that prohibited them from attending Juum'ah, the basic congregational service in their faith. The inmates were in a custody status called "gang minimum," which required them to leave the walled portion of the prison every day to work in gangs outside the institution. Each group of eight to fifteen workers was supervised by one officer.

Under religious law, Juum'ah services only could be held at a specific time, when the gang minimum inmates were outside the facility. A Juum'ah service was held in the prison, but the inmates could not get to it unless excused from their work details and escorted back to the prison.

After problems arose with inmates coming off the work crews and back to the institution at odd times during the day, the institution adopted a rule that said inmates in gang-minimum work would spend all day outside the institution, absent an emergency. Thus, the conflict was created: the inmates wanted to exercise their First Amendment religious beliefs by attending an important religious service. However, the institution did not allow this to happen, citing various reasons, most of which related to security.

The history of *Shabazz* shows why a Supreme Court ruling in this area was needed. The trial court ruled in favor of the institution, relying on a legal test defined earlier by the Third Circuit Court of Appeals. The case then was appealed to the Third Circuit, which decided its earlier case set too easy a standard. The Third Circuit reset its scales, balanced the inmates' rights and institutional interests, and reversed the trial court decision. To justify the restrictions, the institution would have to show not only that the restriction furthered its security interests, but also that no reasonable method existed under which the inmates' religious freedoms could be accommodated.

The Supreme Court disagreed with the approach the court of appeals had taken, and particularly with the "no reasonable method of accommodation" requirement. The Court said: "When a prison regulation impinges on inmates' constitutional rights, the regulation is valid if it is reasonably related to legitimate penological interests." Earlier, and in other decisions, the Court identified legitimate penological interests as including deterrence of crime, rehabilitation of offenders, and institutional security.

The phrase "reasonably related to legitimate penological interests" is vague and subjective. Standing alone, it provides little guidance to persons running correctional facilities. Fortunately, the Court did not stop with this phrase, but went on to spell out a four-step process for applying the test. This process is relatively clear and does provide a blueprint for administrators to use in decisions that may involve the restriction of inmates' constitutional rights.

1. Is there a valid, rational connection (a reasonable or logical connection) between the restriction (in this case, the rule prohibiting some inmates from attending Juum'ah) and "legitimate penological interests" of the institution? In *Shabazz*, the Court found such connections do exist, both in regard to security and rehabilitative interests. The Court emphasized that the judgment calls of officials in this area must be given substantial deference by courts asked to review those judgments.

2. Are there other ways the inmate has of exercising the right in question? In other words, given that the inmates could not attend the religious service, could they exercise their religious beliefs in other ways? Noting the inmates could attend other Muslim services, had access to an Imam (a Muslim religious leader), and were able to have special religious-sensitive diets, the Court found there were alternatives.

3. If the right is accommodated, what impact will that have on staff, other inmates, and on institution resources? Will there be a "ripple effect" on others? The Court found various potentially negative impacts on resources, institution safety, and security. In this area, the Court said that particular deference should be given by lower courts to the judgments and concerns of prison administrators.

4. Finally, the reasonableness of a restriction tends to be shown if there are no ready (obvious, easy) alternatives that would accommodate the inmates' interest at a minimal cost to the institution. Here the Court could see no such alternatives.

After applying each of the four steps to the facts of the *Shabazz* case, the Court upheld the restrictions.

Shabazz actually was the second of two 1987 cases in which the Court announced and applied this test. In the other case, *Turner v. Safley*, regulations prohibiting inmate-to-inmate mail and virtually prohibiting inmate marriages were challenged. Using the same four-step approach, the Court upheld the mail restrictions but overturned the marriage rule. The Court suggested that a more narrowly drawn rule regulating inmate marriages might be satisfactory.

The following are two points about these decisions to keep in mind:

1. The Court clearly rejected any notion that the institution must prove that no reasonable alternative exists that would accommodate an inmate's constitutional interest. The test the Court adopted is a comparatively easy one for the institution to meet.

2. In evaluating an institution's reasons for imposing a restriction, a reviewing court is to give considerable deference to the judgment of correctional officials. It should not second-guess the concerns of officials.

Turner and *Shabazz* Extended

At first, there was some question as to how broadly the "*Turner* test" (as the rule has come to be known) would be applied. An answer to this question came in 1989, when the Court again applied the *Turner* test, this time in a case involving the censorship or rejection of publications sent to an institution.[2]

Under attack were rules of the Federal Bureau of Prisons, which spelled out the circumstances under which an institution could refuse to admit a publication. Typical of these rules was one that prohibited material that "depicts, encourages, or describes methods of escape from correctional facilities . . . ." The court of appeals had thrown out two-thirds of this rule (the "depicts" and "describes" portions) since that court felt publications to be rejected actually must encourage or advocate security breaches, or at least be likely to create such a breach.

The Supreme Court reversed the lower court and held that it had applied too stringent a standard in judging the rules. In reaching this conclusion, the Court overruled a portion of one of its first prison cases, which also dealt with mail rules and which many people felt set the ground rules for any mail restrictions.[3]

The Court limited its earlier decision to dealing with outgoing mail and said the *Turner* test applied to all incoming correspondence, including both publications and letters (except legal mail; *see* Chapter 6). Under the *Turner* test, the rules were valid.

In early 1990, the Court appeared to state clearly that the *Turner* test should be followed in every case that involves trying to balance an inmate's constitutional rights against legitimate penological interests (which will be security, in the great majority of instances).[4]

The case in question, *Washington v. Harper*, dealt with involuntarily medicating mentally ill inmates. It arose under the due process clause of the Fourteenth Amendment. The Court applied the *Turner* test in ruling in favor of the state and said *Turner* applied, no matter what amendment the inmate was suing under, and even if not every part of the four-step approach could be applied.

However, the Court backed away from this very broad application of *Turner* in a 2005 case that involved racial segregation of inmates.[5] In that case, the Court refused to apply *Turner* to evaluate a challenge to California's practice of temporarily segregating inmates by race following their admission or transfer to a prison. Instead, the Court applied the "strict scrutiny" test that is traditionally applied in cases involving racial segregation.

The *Turner* test will continue to be applied in First Amendment cases, to some degree in access-to-the-courts cases, and perhaps in some due process cases.

The following are some examples of cases decided since *Turner* in which institutional restrictions were approved:

1. Two inmates were transferred from a lower to a high security prison based on association with violent extremist groups, where the association had occurred ten years before the transfer. The inmates had done nothing recently to raise concerns about their security. The district court decided officials had exaggerated their response to security concerns, but the court of appeals reversed, approving the transfer.[6]

2. A Jewish inmate attacked a rule limiting beards to no more than one inch. He won the case at the district court before *Turner*. The district court reconsidered the case after *Turner* and again threw out the rule. On appeal, the court of appeals reversed the lower court and upheld the rule.[7]

Case Study: Apply Restrictions Equally, Be Sure of Reasons for Restrictions

Successfully defending a restriction of an inmate's ability to practice his or her religion may depend on whether the policy is enforced consistently. For instance, requiring a Rastafarian to cut his long hair (his "dreadlocks") while allowing Native Americans to wear their hair long was of concern to one court.[8]

> **Another court prescribed similar concerns in a case where the inmate who asserted a religious belief in long hair argued that other religious groups in the institution, including Sikhs and Native Americans, were not required to the cut their hair. The court in that case also was concerned that the defendants produced no evidence to show that the interests they asserted to justify their short hair policy were, in fact, the reasons that the policy was adopted.[9]**

In another case very similar to the *Shabazz* case, a handful of Jewish inmates were not allowed to move between institutions in a prison complex to attend religious services, even though such movement had been allowed in the past without problem. In this case, the court felt there were easy alternatives to what amounted to a total ban on the inmates being able to attend important services and, therefore, required the institution to move the inmates for the services.[10]

Conclusion

The *Turner* version of the balancing test has the effect of presetting the scale a court will use to weigh competing constitutional and institutional interests and to preset that scale somewhat in favor of the institution. In other words, while the institution still will have to convince a reviewing court that a restriction it is imposing furthers a legitimate penological interest, that burden will not be that difficult to meet. Courts generally have heeded the Supreme Court's admonition in *Turner* and *Shabazz* for lower courts to defer to the judgment of correctional administrators. Where courts apply the *Turner* test, institutional interests usually prevail.

Review Questions

1. What is the most common institutional concern that may justify restriction of an inmate's constitutional rights?

2. True or False: The *Turner* test has made it harder for an institution to justify restricting constitutional rights of inmates.

3. The institution imposes a restriction on an inmate practicing his religion. The inmate sues, claiming his First Amendment rights have been violated. The institution responds by saying, "The restriction was imposed because of security needs." Based on this response, will the institution win the lawsuit? Why or why not?

Endnotes

1. *Turner v. Safley*, 107 S.Ct. 2254 (1987). *O'Lone v. Estate of Shabazz*, 107 S.Ct. 2400 (1987).

2. *Thornburgh v. Abbott*, 109 S.Ct. 1874 (1989).

3. *Procunier v. Martinez*, 94 S.Ct. 1800 (1974).

4. *Washington v. Harper*, 449 U.S. 210 (1990); 110 S.Ct. 1028 (1990).

5. *Johnson v. California*, 543 U.S. 499 (2005).

6. *Baraldini v. Thornburgh*, 884 F.2d 615 (D.C. Cir., 1989).

7. *Fromer v. Scully*, 874 F.2d 69 (2d Cir., 1989).

8. *Reed v. Faulkner*, 842 F.2d 906 (2d Cir., 1988).

9. *Swift v. Lewis*, 901 F.2d 730 (9th Cir., 1990).

10. *Whitney v. Brown*, 882 F.2d 1068 (6th Cir., 1989).

Chapter 6:
The First Amendment:
Religion, Mail, Publications,
Visiting, and Expression

The First Amendment to the U.S. Constitution provides freedom of religion, of speech, and of the press.

> Congress shall make no law respecting an establishment of religion, or prohibiting the free exercise thereof, or abridging the freedom of speech, or of the press; or the right of the people peaceably to assemble, and to petition the government for a redress of grievances.

The First Amendment is perhaps the most cherished and fundamental freedom in the Bill of Rights. Freedom of religion, speech, and of the press are recognized as absolutely basic parts of the structure of American society. But even though the First Amendment says no law may be made restricting or abridging the rights guaranteed by the Amendment, over the years, courts have recognized that in certain situations, the government legitimately may restrict rights protected by the First Amendment. In general, such restrictions are very difficult for the government to justify: a "clear and present danger" may have to be shown before the government can prevent someone in the general public from exercising his or her First Amendment rights.

Prior restraint—preventing someone from exercising a right as opposed to responding to the way the right was exercised—is not favored. The purposes of the First Amendment are better served by letting someone make the speech or hold the demonstration and then responding to problems created by those acts than forbidding the acts altogether based on a concern that they might cause problems.

However, because the government's legitimate need to be able to run a safe, secure facility is so important, courts agree that it should be easier to justify a restriction on First Amendment rights inside a correctional institution than it is to justify restrictions on the street. Therefore, a person's First Amendment rights actually are reduced, sometimes very substantially, by the fact of being incarcerated. "Prior restraint" limitations are common in prison.

First Amendment Rights in Prisons and Jails

First Amendment issues, particularly religious questions, were among the first courts addressed in the early days of the hands-on era and remain among the most common subjects of inmate lawsuits today. Congress breathed new life into religious litigation in 2000 when it passed a law known as the "Religious Land Use and Institutionalized Persons Act." In short, "RLUIPA" made it legally more difficult for correctional officials to restrict inmate religious practices. This law is discussed in more detail later in this chapter

Inmates enjoy various First Amendment protections but these protections are considerably less than they would be on the streets. In other words, the institution still must justify a restriction on an inmate's First Amendment rights, but that justification is much easier to make than it would be outside the institution setting.

Most First Amendment issues arise because the way in which the inmate wants to exercise a First Amendment right (such as receipt of a publication or practicing religion in some way) conflicts with some interest of the institution. Courts resolve these conflicts by applying the *Turner* balancing test, described in Chapter 5. Under this approach, a court will approve the decision to restrict an inmate's exercise of a First Amendment right if the court finds the restriction is reasonably related to a "legitimate penological interest" of the institution.[1] Institutional security and safety are the most common "legitimate penological interests" but rehabilitation and deterrence of crime also have been recognized as legitimate penological interests. In some cases, courts accept cost and administrative efficiency as legitimate penological interests.

Religious Issues

Religious issues are probably the most commonly litigated First Amendment issues. In two of its first inmate cases, the Supreme Court recognized that inmates' religious beliefs enjoy at least some First Amendment protections. In one case, the Court reversed a summary dismissal of an Illinois Black Muslim inmate's claim that prison officials refused to allow him to obtain materials about his faith. In a second decision eight years later, the Court said that allegations by a Texas inmate, who claimed officials denied him the opportunity to practice his Buddhist faith, if true, stated a valid claim for relief under the First Amendment.[2] Most cases deal with restrictions the institution places on ways an inmate can practice his religion, but other issues may arise.

Is it a Religion?

In the most common sort of religious case, the inmate says "the prison will *not* let me practice my faith in a certain way." Sometimes, there is a preliminary question presented in such cases: does what the inmate wants to do constitute a religious practice? In these cases, the court must grapple with the question "what is a religion?"

If what the inmate wants to practice is not a religion, then the institution usually will not legally have to justify restrictions, since the practice will not be seen as being protected by the First Amendment. Therefore, sometimes it is in the interest of institution officials to try to decide if something is or is not a religion. However, as the cases discussed below show, courts are reluctant to explore whether a set of beliefs or practices is or is not a religion.

Deciding "what is a religion" is not easy. Courts use different tests for deciding if something is a religion and hence protected by the First Amendment. One court used a somewhat objective test:

> a religion addresses fundamental and ultimate questions having to do with deep and imponderable matters . . . a religion is comprehensive in nature, (consisting) of a belief system as opposed to an isolated teaching . . . religion can often be recognized by the presence of certain formal and external signs.[3]

Another court defined religion as follows:

> . . . the feelings, acts, and experiences of individual men in their solitude, so far as they apprehend themselves to stand in relations to whatever they may consider the divine.[4]

The tests are difficult to understand, let alone apply in a particular situation. Yet, the test a court uses may dictate the result. For instance, the objective test from the *Africa* case cited above in footnote 3 was used in a criminal case in which the defendant claimed he was the Reverend of the Church of Marijuana. He said he sincerely believed that his religion commanded him to use, possess, and distribute marijuana for the benefit of mankind and the planet Earth and that to prosecute him criminally would violate his First Amendment rights. The court said that while he may be sincere in his beliefs, they did not amount to a religion.[5]

But how would this case have been decided if the court had used the more subjective test, where the inquiry is "whether the beliefs professed by a [claimant] are sincerely held and whether they are, in his own scheme of things, religious."?[6]

Another court, applying an objective test which in essence asked "does it look like a religion?" found that witchcraft, as practiced by the Church of Wicca, was a religion and that prison officials would have to justify any restrictions on its practice. The court found various restrictions imposed were justified.[7]

The same test was applied in a case brought by an Arkansas prisoner who described himself as a member of the "Hebrew" religion, although he did not necessarily consider himself Jewish. The focus of his faith was the Old Testament, shorn of what the inmate felt were incorrect Christian interpretations of it. Arkansas officials argued that the inmate's beliefs could not be considered a "religion." The argument failed. His beliefs involved "fundamental and ultimate questions having to do with deep and imponderable matters" and involved a belief system that was "comprehensive in nature." Because the inmate was still trying to figure out where his beliefs fit within various branches of Judaism, the court was not concerned that his faith, in its evolving form, lacked many rituals.[8]

Sometimes the "what is a religion?" question arises in rather contrived situations, such as the inmate who formed the "Church of the New Song" (CONS). Among the early practices of this "religion" was a sacrament requiring the inmate to be served steak and wine from time to time. CONS was the subject of a great deal of litigation through the 1970s, with the courts eventually refusing to grant First Amendment protections to the Church of the New Song. More recently, this inmate was still litigating about something called the Holy Mizanic faith.[9]

Another court ruled that the Universal Life Church, which bestows religious titles ("Doctor of Divinity," and so forth) for a fee by mail, is not a religion.[10]

Given the complexity of deciding whether something is or is not a religion and the lawsuits that may come from deciding something is not a religion, this decision is not one that line staff should make. Just because an officer knows nothing about what an inmate offers as a religion, or the inmate's beliefs are very different from those held by the officer does not mean that what the inmate is trying to practice is not a religion. Regardless of what legal test courts use to decide if something is or is not a religion, they will not attempt to evaluate the merits of what is asserted to be a religion, or whether its beliefs are the "right" ones.

Sincerity of Beliefs

If an inmate is not sincere in his or her religious beliefs, the institution is under no duty to accommodate the inmate's request to practice the religion. There are no easy "litmus tests" for determining an inmate's sincerity.

While it is easy to be skeptical about the sincerity of an inmate's religious beliefs when he makes dramatic religious conversions after entering prison or asks for special accommodations for practices that seem far from the mainstream of his faith, courts assume an inmate's beliefs are sincerely held and put the burden on the institution to show that they are not. This is not an easy burden to meet and the institution should be cautious in rejecting an inmate's request for some religious practice accommodation based on a conclusion that the inmate's beliefs are not sincerely held.

In one case, the court upheld the decision of prison officials to refuse to allow an inmate who said he was a Muslim to have a prayer rug until he also asked for a pork-free diet. In another case, failing to request religious services for twelve years, failing to submit information about the religion to the institution in response to a request, failing to file an administrative appeal about being denied religious services, and the generally ambiguous nature of the alleged religious beliefs all contributed to a finding of insincerity.[11]

Inconsistent and changing requests for religious accommodations can be indicators of insincerity. In a case brought by an inmate who claimed to be a Wotanist (a believer in Norse gods), the court noted that the number of items the inmate wanted to keep in his cell (including boar flesh on holy days) changed. At one point, he said he and the group he was trying to form needed ritual feasts on forty-three different holy days. Later the number dropped to fifteen. He asked for an unspiced diet but wanted to keep herbs and spices in his cell. He claimed various types of meat had spiritual force and that his religion required him to eat meat but then asked for a vegetarian diet. Perhaps the straw that broke the camel's back was the inmate's assertion of his "sincere" belief that his religion required conjugal visits with women "for purposes of sexual magic and divination."[12]

In a case in which the inmate claimed to be Jewish and wanted a kosher diet, a lengthy investigation by prison officials showed that the inmate also had a history of "inconsistent requests and actions," including "several attempts to harass prison officials and disrupt prison life."[13]

When courts interpret "sincerely held religious beliefs" broadly, particularly under RLUIPA, the phrase still has some limits. An inmate demanded a kosher diet as part of his "Orthodox Catholic" faith. In rejecting the claim, the court said that "an inmate's purely subjective ideas of what his religion requires will not suffice." Even RLUIPA requires "the existence of some belief system from which the practice is derived."[14] The court said if the inmate could show, through expert testimony, a link between Orthodox Catholicism and a kosher diet, his claim might survive.

In each of these cases, the facts were complex and the inmates' actions relatively extreme. These decisions indicate that a finding that the inmate is not sincere in his or her professed religious beliefs is likely to be based on a combination of factors.

One factor that courts generally have *not* accepted as indicating insincerity is the fact that the inmate's criminal actions are inconsistent with any sort of religious belief. The inmate's conduct while in prison will be a far more important determining factor about the inmate's sincerity (or lack of sincerity). Like the "what is a religion?" question, decisions that an inmate is not sincere and therefore may be denied permission to practice his or her religion in some way are not decisions that line staff should make.

The Religious Land Use and Institutionalized Persons Act

Litigation over restrictions on religious practices changed after 2000, when Congress passed the Religious Land Use and Institutionalized Persons Act (RLUIPA). That law reflects the belief of Congress that the Supreme Court's interpretation of the First Amendment made it too easy for prison officials to impose restrictions on inmates' religious practices. Congress wanted to replace the institution-friendly *Turner* test as a means of evaluating inmate religious claims with a more difficult test. The result is that now inmates challenge restrictions on their religious practices under two different legal theories: the First Amendment and the somewhat easier requirements of RLUIPA. It is common for a court to find that a restriction on an inmate's religious practice does not violate the First Amendment but does violate RLUIPA.

As its name suggests, portions of RLUIPA deal with land use restrictions that might affect the practice of religion and have no impact on corrections. Zoning laws that restrict the size of a church building would be an example of how RLUIPA would deal with land use issues.

Congress passed a similar law in the 1990s known as the Religious Freedom Restoration Act (RFRA). However, the Supreme Court declared RFRA unconstitutional as applied to state and local governments.[15] RLUIPA is Congress' attempt to correct the flaws that the Supreme Court found in RFRA. The attempt was successful, as the Supreme Court upheld RLUIPA's constitutionality in 2005.[16]

RLUIPA says that any agency receiving federal funding that places a "substantial burden" on any inmate's exercise of religion must justify that restriction by showing the restriction furthers a compelling governmental interest and is the least-restrictive means of doing so. Virtually all state prison systems and probably most jails receive some type of federal funding so there are probably few prisons or jails to which RLUIPA does not apply.

What is a "Substantial Burden?"

The first showings that an inmate must make in either a RLUIPA or First Amendment claim are that the institution has imposed a "substantial burden" on a sincerely held religious belief. (See earlier discussion of "sincerely held beliefs.)

Federal courts are still struggling to reach a consistent definition of "substantial burden," since Congress did not define the phrase in RLUIPA. A starting point is an old Supreme Court decision that said that the government puts a substantial burden on the practice of religion when it puts "substantial pressure on an adherent to modify his behavior and to violate his beliefs."[17]

An almost knee-jerk reaction among many correctional administrators is to define "substantial burden" based on the mandates or core tenets of a religion: "I have no obligation to accommodate Inmate X's religious request if what he is asking for is not mandated by his faith." This reaction is legally incorrect, at least under RLUIPA. In the *Cutter* decision, where the Supreme Court said RLUIPA did not violate the Constitution, the Court also noted that by its terms, RLUIPA makes it clear that a practice need not be "compelled by, or central to, a system of religious belief."[18] Instead, the general rule is that a belief need be only sincere and religious in order to be protected.

Compelling Governmental Interests

Once the inmate has shown the institution has imposed a substantial burden on a sincerely held religious belief, the institution must show (1) that the restriction furthers a compelling governmental interest and (2) that the restriction is the least-restrictive alternative available.

A "compelling governmental interest" is similar to "legitimate penological interests" from the *Turner* test. For example, courts recognize security and discipline as compelling governmental interests. Meeting this part of RLUIPA is not particularly difficult.

Least-Restrictive Alternatives

The second burden, the "least-restrictive alternative" test, can be difficult to meet because it invites a court to second guess the decision of an official. Remember, under the *Turner* test, courts must generally defer to decisions of officials. The "least-restrictive alternative" test means courts will show less deference to the judgment calls of officials.

What one prison system allows is relevant in analyzing whether the restriction under attack is the "least restrictive" alternative. In essence, the court is saying "If some other state allows the religious practice in question, why can't you?"

An example of this arose in a case involving a federal inmate.[19] *Sample* involved an application of the Religious Freedom Restoration Act, which remains applicable to the federal government (*see* endnote 15). The case highlights the contrast between analyzing a religious restriction under the First Amendment versus RLUIPA. Harvey Sample was a federal inmate and an "observant Jew." He sued the Federal Bureau of Prisons for not allowing him to have 3.5 ounces of red wine as part of the Jewish Sabbath and Passover.

Having wine with the activities in question was "an important part of the Jewish religion." The inmate's beliefs were sincerely held.

The first RLUIPA question was whether not allowing the inmate to have wine as part of his Jewish faith imposed a substantial burden on the inmate's religious beliefs. By prohibiting the inmate from exercising his sincerely held religious belief, the court said that the prison had imposed a substantial burden on his religious beliefs.

The court then reached the compelling governmental interest and least-restrictive means questions. Controlling alcohol in a prison furthered various compelling governmental interests but the court said it needed more information before it could decide whether a complete ban on alcoholic beverages was the least-restrictive means for furthering those interests. The Bureau of Prisons' policy gave individual wardens the discretion to allow inmates to consume small amounts of wine in religious rituals under controlled conditions. The warden of Mr. Sample's prison did not allow wine under any circumstances. Officials said that giving wine to one inmate would mean it would have to be given to inmates of other faiths and would "encourage non-Jewish inmates with issues related to chemical dependency to change their religious preference to Jewish, thereby undermining the integrity of the Jewish religious program." and an "administrative nightmare" leading to "chaos in prisons" would be the result. The court felt that these assertions were speculative and not supported by the record and denied the prison officials' motion to dismiss the case.[19]

Had this case been judged using the *Turner* test, the court probably would have deferred to the concerns of the officials and ruled in their favor. Under RLUIPA, the court demanded officials make a clearer showing that their concerns were valid and some accommodation of the inmate's demands was not possible. There have been no further reported decisions in the case that would change its final result.

Particular Religious Issues

Religious Diets. One of the more difficult religious practice issues that has developed over the years is that of religious diets. Prior to RLUIPA, the most common religious diet cases involved pork and were commonly solved when institutions developed pork-free diets for Muslim and Jewish inmates, although there were exceptions. In an early case, a federal appeals court required that an Orthodox Jewish inmate be given a kosher diet.[20] This decision came before the *Turner* test and other courts, applying *Turner*, have not followed *Kahane*. Diet cases have become more difficult under RLUIPA, but court decisions still do not provide clear guidance. Providing inmates with pork free diets may not longer suffice.

Providing a diet that forces an inmate to violate his religious beliefs will be seen as imposing a substantial burden on that inmate's religious faith. But courts also have recognized that circumstances may show there are compelling governmental reasons for not providing a particular religious diet and that there are no less-restrictive alternatives. With some exceptions, the trend of the RLUIPA decisions clearly is in favor of expanding the requirements for accommodating inmate religious diets.

Case Study: Religious Diets and the Religious Land Use and Institutionalized Persons Act

A Seventh Day Adventist inmate in an Oregon prison asked for a kosher diet. Kosher meals were available for Jewish inmates. His request was denied and the inmate filed a suit under the Religious Land Use and Institutionalized Persons Act. The defendants argued he was not entitled to any relief for several reasons. They said the Seventh Day Adventist faith does not require its adherents to eat kosher meals, although they conceded that some Adventists believe a kosher diet is consistent with their religious beliefs. An affidavit from the prison's religious coordinator expressed the concern that if one Adventist inmate received a kosher diet, then the 2,700 other Adventists in the prison system would want one and that providing that many meals would cost the state an extra $5.5 million every year.

The court rejected the arguments of the officials and entered a preliminary injunction that allowed the inmate to receive kosher meals at least through a complete trial on the merits. There have been no other reported decisions in the case since 2008, suggesting it has been resolved.

Citing language from RLUIPA, the court pointed out that inmates do not have to show that a particular religious practice is required by their organized faith to at least potentially be entitled to relief under the law. The focus is not on what the organized church requires, but what the individual's sincerely held religious beliefs are.

Forcing the inmate to choose between eating a diet he believed was forbidden by his faith (as he defined the requirements of the faith) or changing his religious affiliation to Jewish to get kosher meals put a substantial burden on the exercise of his religion.

While the state had a compelling governmental interest in maintaining an efficient food service, the religious coordinator was not qualified to discuss the costs of providing meals since he was not involved in food service management or procurement. There was no indication the defendants had actually tried to assess the demand for kosher meals among the Adventist inmate population so the coordinator's speculation about 2,700 Adventist inmates lining up for kosher meals was not convincing.

> **Finally, officials argued that providing a kosher diet just to Jewish inmates was the least-restrictive means they had of limiting food costs. However, there was no evidence that they had considered other alternatives. Therefore, the court said, the officials failed to meet their burden of showing limiting kosher meals to just Jewish inmates was their least-restrictive means of limiting costs.** *Wofford v. Williams*, **2008 U.S. Dist. Lexis 63946 (D.Or., 2008).**

The cost of providing a special diet can provide a "compelling governmental interest" under RLUIPA for not providing the diet, but the burden will be on the institution to show the fiscal impact of providing the diet. How the court "computes" the cost can produce very different results.

A kosher diet costs more to provide than a "regular" prison diet. One court focused on the extra cost per meal to provide a kosher diet, found the extra cost would put a great strain on the food budget of the Texas Department of Criminal Justice, and decided that RLUIPA did not require kosher diets. Another court looked at the estimated total annual extra cost of providing kosher meals in comparison to the Colorado prison system's total food budget and decided that it would amount to only 0.158% of that budget, a minimal impact. It rejected costs as a justification for not providing kosher meals.[21]

Another argument against providing a special diet is that doing so will create a security risk because other inmates will see the diet as favoritism. The *Baranowski* decision cited in the previous footnote accepted the assertions of officials that providing kosher meals would breed resentment and relied on that concern to at least some degree in its holding that Texas officials did not have to provide kosher meals.

However, a Massachusetts district court rejected the same argument from prison officials where the record showed very little evidence that providing special meals for Muslim inmates would produce conflict between inmate groups. It noted that the Bureau of Prisons had been providing Muslims with special meals for a decade without problem and that the Massachusetts Department of Corrections (where the case arose) provided dietary accommodations for Jewish, Buddhist, and Seventh Day Adventist groups and could show only one example of friction as a result.[22]

The message from these cases and others is that courts are apt to be skeptical of assertions about security threats, exorbitant costs, and thousands of inmates lining up for special diets so officials should try to support these concerns with more than speculation.

The bottom line regarding religious diets is that an inmate presumptively should be allowed a diet consistent with his religious beliefs. However, if providing the diet creates undue financial and administrative demands, the institution may not have to provide the special diet. There are not enough court decisions that have addressed this issue to clearly show where lines regarding financial or administrative demands are drawn. [23]

Faith-Based Programs

Faith-based programs have received a good deal of attention in the early years of the twenty-first century. This interest extends to such programs in prisons and jails. However, when the government spends money in support of religious activities, there is a risk that the First Amendment Establishment Clause will be violated. The "Establishment Clause" says that government may "make no law respecting the establishment of religion." Some types of government aid to religious organizations are permissible, but others are not. In an extreme example, a prison's attempt to convert all inmates to a particular religious faith as a condition of parole would unquestionably be seen as an attempt to "impermissibly advance" religion and be a violation of the Establishment Clause. Key factors in deciding whether a program has stepped over the line to the point of impermissibly advancing religion include:

1. Did the aid result in governmental indoctrination?

2. Did the government define the recipients of its financial assistance by religion?

3. Is there excessive entanglement between the government and the religious program? [24]

In the *Americans United* case cited in the prior footnote, a program in an Iowa prison failed these tests. The Department of Corrections contracted with a religious group to provide an impressive array of rehabilitative programs in a special housing unit at a very low cost. The legal problem arose because the very focused religious message of the private group permeated virtually every aspect of the unit, including all but one of the rehabilitative programs (computer programming).

While in theory the program was open to any inmate, inmates who were not willing to participate in the evangelical Christian program were effectively precluded from participating. In essence, the State of Iowa was paying for a program for evangelical Christians.

The *Americans United* decision is ground-breaking in that it is the first court of appeals decision that examined an intensely religious faith-based program in a prison setting. The court did not say that all faith-based programs violated the First Amendment, but the decision raises red flags for administrators who are operating or considering faith-based programs.

State-Paid Chaplains

Another example of where correctional facilities have potential Establishment Clause problems is with the hiring of chaplains. Courts have approved this practice, reasoning that where the state imposes burdens on persons freely practicing their religion (by incarcerating them or sending them around the world in the military), the state may compensate by spending money for religious purposes.[25] If state-paid chaplains actively proselytize inmates to join a particular faith, this could be seen as violating the prohibition against the state establishing a religion.

Allocation of Resources

A large institution may have inmates belonging to a large number of different religious faiths. Must resources be allocated equally between these various groups, even though some groups may have a large number of adherents while others may have relatively few members? So long as the groups have a reasonable opportunity to practice their religions, courts have not held equality of treatment is required.[26] This permits an institution to hire a chaplain or chaplains to work with its largest faith groups without having to hire chaplains for every faith group.

Mail and Publications

Rejecting Incoming Mail

In 1989, the Supreme Court decided *Abbott v. Thornburgh*, a case dealing with another First Amendment issue: the censorship or rejection of incoming mail. Several lower courts had decided that to censor or reject publications, the institution had to show the material actually advocated some sort of security breach or was likely to cause a breach.

69

Thus, one court had thrown out rules of the Federal Bureau of Prisons, which allowed material to be rejected that "depicted or described" such things as methods of escape or activities that may lead to the use of physical violence or group disruption. The court did so by relying on a 1974 Supreme Court decision, which it felt controlled the issue.[27]

Again, the Supreme Court reversed the lower court and upheld the rule. The Court limited its 1974 case only to outgoing correspondence and said that for publications and other general (nonlegal) correspondence, the *Turner* test would apply. In other words, if censorship or rejection of a publication was "reasonably related to a legitimate penological objective," the restriction would be valid.

Now, incoming correspondence is judged by the same standard that applies to restrictions on such things as inmates' attempts to practice their religion, which in some way may conflict with legitimate institutional interests (such as security and rehabilitation). Another important aspect of the Supreme Court's 1989 publication censorship case was the Court's holding that when any part of a publication was properly rejected, the entire issue of the publication could be rejected. Institution officials do not have to cut and paste magazines to review objectionable parts and deliver what is left.

The Mail-Restriction Rule Applied

There have not been many publication-rejection decisions since the Supreme Court's decision in the *Abbott* case.[27] Racist literature, which could fan the flames of racial unrest in an institution, generally can be banned. At least some types of sexual publications also can be banned, but a ban on all sexually oriented publications may go too far. See discussion of sexually oriented publications, below.

A ban on pretrial detainees receiving any publications in the mail was upheld in one case, in part because of the relatively short time a detainee is likely to be in jail.[28]

Publication censorship decisions remain a very sensitive legal area. Agency rules and policies need to be drafted carefully, and the actual decision to reject a publication needs to be made by an official who understands the rules and their importance. The decision to reject a publication or a letter normally would not be made by line staff.

Due Process and Rejection

Rejection of publications or letters, either incoming or outgoing, also raises a due process issue. To help assure that rejection decisions are made fairly and according to proper standards, the Supreme Court requires the following when a publication or letter is rejected:

- The inmate must be given notice of the rejection (regardless of whether the inmate was the sender or the intended recipient of the letter).

- The author of the letter must be given an opportunity to protest the censorship decision to an official other than the person who made the original decision to reject the correspondence. This obviously requires that notice of the rejection also be given to the sender of the letter, if the sender is not an inmate.[29] The same requirements apply when a publication is censored. The publication must be given a notice of the rejection and an opportunity to protest that decision.[30]

Test for Outgoing Mail

While the Supreme Court created a new test for restricting incoming mail in the *Abbott* case, it left the test for outgoing mail unchanged because the Court felt as a general rule that outgoing mail presents substantially less of a security threat than does incoming mail. To reject a piece of outgoing mail, a stronger case must be made showing that the letter threatens security or rehabilitation and that there are no less-restrictive alternative ways of responding to this threat other than refusing to mail the letter.

Facility policy should indicate the grounds for rejecting publications or letters and the procedure that should be followed in making such decisions. These policies should be followed carefully and rejection decisions carefully documented.

Legal Mail

Special requirements apply to mail to inmates from attorneys, the courts, and other government officials (legal mail). Such mail may be protected by a legal privilege (as with attorney-client mail) as well as by the Constitution. Therefore, such mail normally cannot be read by institution staff and should be opened only in the presence of the inmate and examined at that point for contraband.

Media Mail

Does mail between an inmate and the media (TV or radio stations, newspaper reporters, and so forth) have a special status, like legal mail? Although a 1978 case from Texas did hold that media mail was "privileged" and must be handled with the same precautions as legal mail, more recent cases have rejected that ruling and criticized it. Therefore, most courts probably would hold that media mail is entitled to no special privileges, but may be treated as any other normal type of mail. [31]

Publishers-Only Rules

Rules requiring that books and other publications be sent to inmates only from publishers (publishers-only rules) have been upheld as furthering valid security concerns.[32] A publishers-only rule was seen as a preferable alternative to a jail's policy of banning all hardbound books, even when they came from a publisher. Another alternative the court said would have been acceptable was for the institution to tear the covers off the books. But a total ban (particularly when combined with the lack of any library facilities or softbound books) was unconstitutional for an inmate held in a jail nearly 1,000 days who was seeking literature on alcoholism.[33]

Sexual Publications

Sexually oriented publications can be banned from correctional facilities. While courts are still examining the details about acceptable regulations and how closely the federal courts will examine regulations, the weight of authority suggests that regulations that allow bans of publications need to be drafted carefully and officials should be able to demonstrate the rational connection between a ban and legitimate penological interests under the *Turner* test.

The *Cline* case, discussed in the previous chapter, provides an examples of a rule that was drafted too broadly, so that it apparently banned books up to and including the Bible because they included sexual passages, an interpretation of the rule by an official that expanded its already overbroad scope, and an overreaction by prison officials that took more than 20 percent of the books out of the prison library because somewhere in them might be a sentence or two that could be a "sexual turn-on."

A ban on popular magazines such as *Playboy,* which include nude photographs, has been approved.[34] In one of these cases, the rule banned pictures showing "frontal nudity." In the other, the rules were carefully written to ban pornography while recognizing that not all photographs of nudity are pornographic (such as the *National Geographic* or photos of many great works of art).

In a more recent case, *Strope v. Collins,*[35] the court questioned whether banning a magazine because it contained "a few photographs of women's partially bare buttocks" was rationally related to legitimate penological interests. In *Strope,* the district court judge denied the parties' cross-motions for summary judgment, saying he wanted to hear more evidence about the justification for the rule.

Strope highlights two closely related concerns courts are apt to have about bans on publications. The first is whether the regulation that officials rely upon to justify their actions is over broad. Here a court will evaluate the rule "as written," and consider what its language literally applies to. Does it prohibit innocuous materials (*National Geographic*) along with objectionable ones (*Hustler*)? If a rule bans descriptions of sexual intercourse, would a book that described a King seeing a beautiful woman, having her brought to him and "laying with her," and leaving her pregnant be banned? If so, good-bye Bible.[36]

The second question is whether there is a rational connection between the rule and specifically what was banned. Here courts look at the rule "as applied" and may demand expert testimony to justify what legitimate penological interests are furthered by the rule. The defendants in the *Strope* case did not offer such expert testimony and were not able to wiggle out of the case on summary judgment. They may ultimately win after a full trial. By contrast, the defendants in another case offered detailed expert testimony to support a carefully drafted regulation and the court accepted the testimony and upheld the rule.[37]

To make matters even more confusing, the Tenth Circuit Court of Appeals approved a jail's rule that banned "sexually explicit" material and "technical publications," even though the rule did not define either term. There was no expert testimony offered to justify the rule, only a jail lieutenant's assertion that the jail had a "fair amount" of sexual assaults and that sexually explicit material "may inflame a prisoner, excite a prisoner, perhaps assault another prisoner, force him to perform a sex act."[38]

Visiting

Correctional professionals uniformly recognize the importance of visiting in both prisons and jails. However, on several occasions, the Supreme Court has refused to hold that at least due process (part of the Fourteenth Amendment) guarantees inmates an unfettered right to visits.[40]

In the *Bazzetta* case (*see* endnote 39), the issue of whether inmates had a constitutional right to visits came to the court. The Michigan Department of Corrections had adopted several very rigorous restrictions on visits. For instance, inmates' siblings under the age of eighteen could not visit. Inmates found guilty of two or more substance abuse infractions permanently lost all visiting opportunities, although they could request reinstatement of visits after two years. The Court of Appeals for the Sixth Circuit held that inmates had a limited right to association that included a right to non-contact visits. This right to visit was subject to restriction under the *Turner* test. It then overturned several of the regulations, saying these were not reasonably related to legitimate penological interests.

The Supreme Court reversed. The Court specifically shied away from discussing the extent to which inmates may have a right of association or the scope of that right. Instead, the Court assumed there was such a right and said the regulations in question met the *Turner* test.

The case does not blaze new ground but strongly reaffirms the Supreme Court's position of the last several years that federal courts should be reluctant to overturn prison rules even when those rules may restrict constitutionally protected inmate rights.

In upholding the regulations, the Court made two general statements of importance. The first was to again emphasized that courts must "accord substantial deference to the professional judgment of prison administrators" in issues relating to "defining the legitimate goals of a corrections system and for determining the most appropriate means to accomplish them."[41] It also said that when prison regulations are challenged as violating the Constitution, prison officials do not have the burden of proving the validity of the regulations, but those attacking the rules have the legal burden of showing the rules are not valid.

The Supreme Court has also twice held that inmates do not have any right to contact visits.[42] If there is no right to contact visiting, there also obviously is no right to conjugal visiting, although some correctional facilities allow conjugal visiting as a matter of policy.

Breastfeeding

Several years ago, a couple of courts considered the question of whether female inmates have a right to breastfeed their infants. The general answer is probably "no," but under somewhat unique circumstances, one court said that an institution at least had to allow a woman to breastfeed her baby in the visiting room, when the mother and child otherwise would have been together. The court noted that mothers were allowed to bottle feed their babies during regular visits and could see no reason not to allow breastfeeding under the same circumstances. Even in this case, the court refused to require the institution to store or otherwise handle the mother's milk.[43] The issue of breastfeeding has not been discussed in reported decisions in recent years.

Telephone Calls

Years ago, inmates rarely were allowed to make telephone calls, except the "call to my lawyer" at booking and in emergency situations. With the advent of technology that allows greater control over calls and the ability of institutions to make money from inmate telephone systems, telephones are common in prison dayrooms across the country.

Consistent with the general right of association that the Supreme Court assumed existed in the 2003 *Bazzetta* decision (*see* Visiting, above), most courts still stop short of saying that inmates have a per se right to use a telephone, although providing telephones is one means prison officials have of facilitating inmates' general right to communicate. In any event, telephone access is subject to limitations and controls based on reasonable security and administrative concerns of the institution.[44]

At least where inmates are advised that their telephone calls will be monitored, they have no constitutional right to privacy that protects their calls nor does monitoring violate their rights under federal wiretapping laws. Thus, statements made in phone calls may be used by institutional officials and may be introduced against the inmate in criminal trials.[45]

Association and Group Activities

Institution officials have almost complete authority to restrict or prohibit inmate group activities. Inmates in the North Carolina prison system attempted to form a prisoners' union, hold meetings, and prepare and distribute written literature. Prison officials barred such activity even though they limited the inmates' ability to exercise their First Amendment rights of speech and association. The Supreme Court approved the actions of the officials, noting that speech rights were barely implicated and that associational rights were curtailed "by the realities of confinement."[46] Unless the security concerns of the officials could be shown conclusively to be wrong, they should prevail.

Conclusion

While courts are more willing to side with the institution in dealing with First Amendment questions than they have been in years past, First Amendment issues remain legally sensitive. Staff should be aware when they are dealing with First Amendment issues and act with care in those areas.

Review Questions

1. What is the most common justification for restricting inmates' First Amendment rights?

2. In general terms, what is the major difference between the legal test imposed by the First Amendment for evaluation of a restriction on an inmate's ability to practice his or her religion and the legal test imposed by the Religious Land Use and Institutionalized Persons Act?

3. Since the beginning of the twenty-first century, has the Supreme Court stepped back from its long-held position that lower courts must give substantial deference to judgment calls of correctional officials about such things as institutional safety and security?

Endnotes

[1.] *Turner v. Safley*, 107 S.Ct. 2254 (1987). *O'Lone v. Estate of Shabazz*, 107 S.Ct. 2400 (1987).

[2.] *Cooper v. Pate*, 378 U.S. 546 (1964), *Cruz v. Beto*, 405 U.S. 318 (1972).

[3.] *Africa v. Commonwealth of Pennsylvania*, 662 F.2d 1025, 1032 (3rd Cir., 1981).

[4.] *Patrick v. Lefevre*, 745 F.2d 153, 158 (2d Cir., 1984).

[5.] *U.S. v. Meyers*, 95 F.3d 1475 (10th Cir., 1996).

[6.] *Jackson v. Mann*, 196 F.3d 316, 320 (2d Cir., 1999).

[7.] *Dettmer v. Landon*, 799 F.2d 929 (4th Cir., 1986).

[8] *Love v. Reed*, 216 F.3d 682 (8th Cir., 2000).

[9] *Theriault v. A Religious Office*, 895 F.2d 104 (2d Cir., 1990). This case also cites many of the "CONS" decisions.

[10] *Jones v. Bradley*, 590 F.2d 294 (9th Cir., 1979).

[11] *Vaughn v. Garrison*, 534 F.Supp. 90 (E.D. La., 1981). *Childs v. Duckworth*, 509 F.Supp. 1254 (N.D. Ind., 1981).

[12] *Lindell v. Casperson*, 360 F.Supp. 2d 932, 953 (W.D.Wis, 2005).

[13] *Procknow v. Schueler*, 2006 WL 3054317 (E.D.Wis., 2006) *22.

[14] *Guzzi v. Thompson*, 470 F. Supp. 2d 17. 27 (D,Mass, 2007).

[15] *City of Flores v. Boerne*, 521 U.S. 507 (1997).

[16] *Cutter v. Wilkinson*, 544 U.S. 709 (2005).

[17] *Thomas v. Board of Indiana Employment Security Division*, 450 U.S. 707 (1981).

[18] 42 U.S.C. § 2000cc-5(7)(a).

[19] *Sample v. Lappin*, 479 F.Supp. 2d 120 (D.D.C., 2007. Sample involved an application of the Religious Freedom Restoration Act. The Supreme Court decision finding that act unconstitutional dealt only with the Act's applicability to state and local governments. It remains applicable to federal agencies. See endnote 15.

[20] *Kahane v. Carlson*, 527 F.2d 492 (2d Cir.,1975). This decision came before the *Turner* test and other courts, applying *Turner*, have not followed *Kahane*. See *Cooper v. Rogers*, 788 F. Supp. 255 (D. Md., 1991).

[21] *Baranowski v. Hart*, 486 F.3d 112 (5th Cir., 2007), *Beerheide v. Suthers*, 286 F.3d 1179 (10th Cir., 2002).

[22] *Hudson v. Dennehy*, 2008 U.S. Dist. Lexis 16672.

[23] *Udey v. Kastner*, 805 F.2d 1218 (5th Cir., 1986).

[24] *Americans United for Separation v. Prison Fellowship*, 509 F.3d 406 (8th Cir., 2007).

[25] *Theriault v. Silber*, 547 F.2d 1279 (5th Cir., 1977), cert denied, 98 S.Ct. 216 (1977).

[26] *Thompson v. Commonwealth of Kentucky*, 712 F.2d 1078 (6th Cir., 1983).

[27] *Abbott v. Thornburgh*, 824 F.2d 1166 (D.C. Cir., 1987), reversed, *Thornburgh v. Abbott*, 109 S.Ct. 1874 (1989). The earlier case relied upon was *Procunier v. Martinez*, 94 S.Ct. 1800 (1974).

[28] *Hause v. Vaught*, 993 F.2d 1079 (4th Cir., 1993).

[29] *Procunier v. Martinez*, 94 S.Ct. 1800 (1974).

[30] *Montcalm Pub. Corp. v. Beck*, 80 F.3d 105 (4th Cir., 1996), *Jacklovich v. Simmons*, 392 F.3d 420 (10th Cir., 2004).

[31] *Guajuardo v. Estelle*, 580 F.2d 748 (5th Cir., 1978), but see *Mann v. Adams*, 846 F.2d 591 (9th Cir., 1988), criticizing the reasoning and conclusion in *Guajuardo*, and *Gaines v. Lane*, 790 F.2d 1299 (7th Cir., 1986), also holding media mail is not privileged in any way.

[32] *Bell v. Wolfish*, 441 U.S. 520 (1979).

[33] *Jackson v. Elrod*, 881 F.2d 441 (7th Cir., 1989).

[34] *Mauro v. Arpiao*, 188 F.3d 1054 (9th Cir.,1999), *Amatel v. Reno*, 156 F.3d 192 (D.C. Cir., 1998).

[35] *Strope v. Collins*, 492 F.Supp. 2d 1289 (D.Kan., 2007).

[36] See 2 Sam., 11:1-5.

[37] *Ramirez v. Pugh*, 486 F.Supp. 2d 421 (M.D. Pa., 2007). The rule under attack was the same rule that was upheld in the *Amatel* case (see endnote 34) by a different circuit court of appeals. In *Ramirez*, the Third Circuit had earlier said, in essence, "with all due respect to our colleagues in the District of Columbia Circuit, we think more of an evidentiary showing is needed to uphold that rule than they felt necessary." *Ramirez v. Pugh*, 379 F.3d 122 (3rd Cir., 2004). The 2007 district court decision in *Ramirez* was the result. This shows how one circuit court of appeals can disagree with another.

[38] *Jones v. Salt Lake County*, 503 F.3d 1147 (10th Cir., 2007).

[39] *Bazzetta v. Overton*, 123 S.Ct. 2162 (2003), *Kentucky v. Thompson*, 109 S.Ct. 1904 (1989), *Bell v. Wolfish*, 441 U.S. 520 (1979), *Block v. Rutherford*, 104 S.Ct. 3227 (1984).

[40] 123 S.Ct. 2162 (2003).

[41] *Bell, Block*, supra, n. 29.

[42] Breastfeeding not required, *Sutherland v. Thigpen*, 784 F.2d 713 (5th Cir., 1986). Breastfeeding required during visits, *Berrios-Berrios v. Thornburgh*, 716 F.Supp. 989 (E.D. Ky, 1989).

[43] *Harrison v. Federal Bureau or Prisons*, 464 F.Supp. 2d 552 (E.D.Va., 2006), *Valdez v. Robinson* , 302 F.3d 1039 (9th Cir., 2002).

[44] *United States v. Sababu*, 891 F.2d 1308 (7th Cir., 1989).

[45] *Jones v. North Carolina Prisoners' Labor Union*, 433 U.S. 119 (1977).

Chapter 7:
The Fourth Amendment:
Searches and Seizures

The Fourth Amendment provides, in part, security from unwarrantable search and seizure:

> The right of the people to be secure in their persons, houses, papers, and effects, against unreasonable searches and seizures, shall not be violated . . .

In plain English, the Fourth Amendment means the government cannot conduct *unreasonable* searches or seizures. What an "unreasonable" search is varies. At one extreme, law enforcement officers usually cannot search the person or home of a member of the general public without a search warrant, a document issued by a judicial officer that grants permission for the search and verifies that the judicial officer has been convinced that "probable cause" exists to provide justification for the search. At the other extreme, corrections officials may strip search inmates returning from contact visits without a warrant and without any particular suspicion that an inmate is smuggling contraband.

One major difference between searches conducted by law enforcement officials on the street and those conducted by correctional staff inside the prison or jail is that there is no requirement that institutional searches be accompanied by a search warrant.

The Balancing Test

In general terms, courts determine the reasonableness of a type of search by balancing the degree to which the search intrudes into a person's reasonable expectation of privacy against the government's need for the search. The greater the need, the greater the intrusion is acceptable.

The tragic events of 9-11 provide an example of the balancing test in action. Because of the heightened concern over airline hijackings and terrorism, we accept searches at large public gatherings and at airline terminals—including full body scanning—that probably would have been unconstitutional in simpler times. Yet, because of the government's interest in thwarting terrorist activities, the searches are legally acceptable. However, there are still limits.

As with many other areas of inmates' rights, deciding what a "reasonable" inmate search is involves a balancing test. In applying the balancing test, a court generally asks three basic questions. The first two are whether the person being searched has a subjective (personal) expectation of privacy and then whether society is prepared to recognize that expectation of privacy as reasonable. In other words, does society attach an objective expectation of privacy to the type of search conducted. If the answer to either of these questions is "no," then the person has no Fourth Amendment protections. Courts generally have held that inmates have at least some limited expectations of privacy. However, these expectations are substantially less than persons in the free community have.

Assuming the person has some reasonable expectations of privacy, then the third question arises: does the government have a strong enough reason for conducting the search to justify intruding into the reasonable expectation of privacy the person enjoys? This is where the balancing of inmate rights and institution interests takes place. The more intrusive a search is, the greater the expectation of privacy will be and the greater the justification the government must show.

Many years ago, the Supreme Court set out factors that courts should consider in evaluating whether types of searches are reasonable and whether a specific search was reasonable.

1. The scope of the intrusion. A strip search is much more intrusive than a cell search.

2. The manner in which the search is conducted. This speaks to the professionalism of the officer or officers who conducted the search because this professionalism includes respecting the dignity and privacy of the person being searched and not unnecessarily reducing either of those principles.

3. The justification for the search. The greater the intrusion, the greater the justification for the search must be.

4. The place where the search takes place. This relates to the manner in which the search is conducted.[1]

A correctional officer should conduct searches in a professional, nondegrading way. Unprofessional behavior can include such things as making rude, insulting, or demeaning remarks to the inmate during the search, or performing the search in a way or in a place that unnecessarily exposes the inmate to view by others not involved with the search.

"Reasonable Suspicion:" What Is It?

Given that warrants are typically not required for searches of inmates, one of the major questions courts have addressed when evaluating different types of searches, which occur in a correctional facility is whether a search can be done randomly, without any particular reason to suspect an inmate is carrying contraband, or whether some reason exists to suspect a particular inmate may be carrying contraband. This is referred to as "particularized suspicion" and where it is necessary to justify a given category of searches, courts ask if "reasonable suspicion" existed.

Probably the most controversial and often-litigated type of inmate search where reasonable suspicion is required is strip searches of persons being booked into jails. This is discussed in greater detail later in the chapter.

The phrase "reasonable suspicion" needs to be understood because it has a relatively specific meaning to a court. *Reasonable suspicion* (or *"reasonable belief"*) is a low level of "cause" for a search (*"probable cause"* is a somewhat higher level of cause).

1. The suspicion usually must be focused on the person to be searched. In other words, the cause must be "particularized." Courts have acknowledged that reasonable suspicion can come from more generalized circumstances in the prison/jail context. Agency search policies should provide guidance in this area.

2. There must be a specific fact, combined with the reasonable inferences that can be drawn from the fact in light of experience, for reasonable suspicion to exist. (Fact + judgment = reasonable suspicion.)

Examples of reasonable suspicion cases include the following:

• Where evidence showed two officers were seen smoking next to a fence and marijuana later was smelled, there was no reasonable suspicion justifying searches of the officers.

• Where informant information was received from a person who had no prior record of providing reliable information and there was nothing else to corroborate the information, no reasonable suspicion existed.

- Where an inmate informant and other officers reported on the smuggling conduct of an officer and large amounts of contraband were entering the facility, reasonable suspicion did exist.[2] Anonymous tips alone will not create reasonable suspicion.

In general, "reasonable suspicion" searches demand that suspicion be focused on a single individual. When relying on informant tips, the informant should be reliable. The suspicion must come from some sort of objective fact, not just a hunch. Tips from anonymous informants, without more evidence, are generally not sufficient to provide reasonable suspicion.

Because determining the existence of reasonable suspicion involves a judgment call, it is impossible to provide a written definition of reasonable suspicion that will allow the officer trying to make the determination of whether reasonable suspicion exists in a particular situation do so with total confidence.

Case Study: Strip Searches Approved, but Not Verbal Harassment

Inmates in the segregation unit at the Iowa State Penitentiary were strip searched every time they moved in or out of the unit. All inmates were strip searched before and after contact visits. This included visits with lawyers, clergy, and the prison ombudsman and before and after going to medical facilities, court appearances, or exercise areas.

The district court entered an injunction against the lawyer and medical visit searches, since the court believed some inmates were discouraged from exercising their constitutional rights to attorney visits and medical care because of their distaste for the strip searches. The court of appeals reversed the lower court and upheld the searches, noting from testimony and other sources that inmates often attempt to smuggle contraband in body cavities and that officials had strong security concerns justifying the searches.

However, the court of appeals upheld one portion of the district court's injunction. The lower court had found that some officers, in some situations, accompanied strip searches with "teasing, rude and offensive comments, and other verbal harassment." An injunction prohibiting such conduct was upheld, the court saying "[verbal harassment] is demeaning and bears no relationship to the prison's legitimate security needs." *Goff v. Nix*, 803 F.2d 358 (8th Cir., 1986).

Where any type of search, but particularly a strip or body cavity probe search, is done only after someone decides there is sufficient reason to conduct such a search (reasonable suspicion), the basis for the search should be documented. Such documentation then can provide the basis either for the agency administration to review the decision or the basis for defending the decision in court, should a lawsuit be filed. If the officer or supervisor making the decision does not document the reason, the reason may be forgotten and the search impossible to justify in court. The testimony in court in such a case might go something like this:

Lawyer for the plaintiff: Sergeant Harris, did you approve strip searching my client?

Sgt. Harris: According to the shift log, yes.

Lawyer: Your agency's rules require a finding of reasonable suspicion as a condition to strip search someone. What was the reasonable suspicion in this case?

Sgt. Harris: I don't remember.

Judge (later): The law requires reasonable suspicion for this type of search. It is the institution's burden in this case to show there was reasonable suspicion. Since Sergeant Harris cannot remember why he ordered the search, I find there was no reasonable suspicion and rule for the plaintiff.

Searches in Prison and Jails

Maintaining security is basic to running a prison or jail. The threat to security caused by contraband smuggled into the facility and/or carried by inmates in the facility is obvious and well recognized by the courts. Therefore, the courts accept the compelling need for security as justification to reduce the scope of the Fourth Amendment's protections inside the institution to far less than they are outside. However, this does not mean that no protections exist. The extent of the protections that exist for inmates increases as the searches become more intrusive.

Cell Searches

The Supreme Court has held that inmates simply have no expectation of privacy in their cells, and, therefore, the Fourth Amendment does not even apply to cell searches. Cell searches then may be conducted at random, without any sort of cause or suspicion needed to justify searching a particular cell.[3] The Court also has ruled that inmates have no right to be present when their cells are searched.[4]

Pat Down Searches

The courts also generally have upheld the reasonableness of pat down searches being done randomly. Again, if it can be shown that pat downs are being done to harass particular inmates and are not being done for a legitimate institutional purpose, a court may intervene. Cross-gender pat searches may present special problems (*see* page 93).

Urine Tests

Random urine tests for inmates, while seen as a form of search, have been approved by the courts. Again, the way the urine sample is obtained could be seen as unreasonable, if it exposes the inmate to unnecessary humiliation. If staff observe the inmate providing the urine sample, the staff actually doing the observation should be the same sex as the inmate. This is a good example of an objective expectation of privacy: society generally believes that persons reasonably expect they will not be observed urinating by a person of the opposite sex.

Strip Searches

The Supreme Court reluctantly has approved strip searches of all inmates following their exposure to the opportunity to obtain contraband, such as after a contact visit or trip to a hospital.[5] Courts also have approved strip searching inmates when they leave segregation unit cells because of the especially great security concerns those units present.[6]

Surprisingly, there has been almost no recent litigation regarding strip searching inmates in the general population of an institution at other times. Most facilities restrict such strip searches to circumstances when there is reasonable suspicion that the inmate may be concealing contraband.

In one case, a district court approved a policy under which two cells were selected at random every day to be thoroughly searched. These searches included strip searches of the inmates housed in the cells.[7]

Agency policy should address when inmates may be strip searched. Because of the legal sensitivity of strip searches, staff should follow such policies with care. Particular attention should be paid to documenting the need for a strip search when the search is based on a discretionary decision.

Jail Strip Searches

Jails face a unique strip-search issue that prisons do not: deciding under what circumstances arrestees can be strip searched as part of the admissions process to the jail.

With only one exception, discussed below, courts across the country have held that automatic strip searches of persons arrested and booked for minor offenses are unreasonable and violate the Fourth Amendment.[8] Arrestee strip search cases began in the early 1980s and the reasonable suspicion rule was applied from the beginning. Despite the overwhelming body of case law, many jails continued to strip search all arrestees, leading to a dramatic surge of

Case Study: Second Strip Search Crosses the Line

Following a stabbing in the prison, correctional officers were shaking down all inmates and their cells. An inmate was strip searched as part of the shakedown. Only moments after the search, he was handcuffed and removed from his cell. Shortly thereafter, he was then strip searched a second time. The inmate alleged that officers struck him several times and were verbally abusive during the second search. Were these searches reasonable? (The case came before the court on a motion to dismiss, so the court had to accept the plaintiff's allegations as true.)

The first search, as part of the larger response to the stabbing was reasonable. Assuming the plaintiff could prove his allegations about never being out of sight of the officers, the second search had no legitimate penological purpose and was unreasonable. The court said the physical and verbal abuse, if true, helped show the second search was intended to harass and intimidate the inmate. *Jean-Laurent v. Wilkinson,* 2006 WL 1880356 (S.D.N.Y., 2006).

litigation during the first decade of the twenty-first century. These recent cases have typically resulted in substantial amounts of damages, sometimes millions of dollars, paid to the arrestees. As an example, a county with a forty-five to sixty bed jail bitterly contested an arrestee strip search case. After almost five years of litigation, sixteen reported decisions and a complete loss on the legal merits, the case was settled for $3,000,000.[9] This result is common.

Except in the Ninth and Eleventh Circuits (the far west and southeast),[10] courts say that reasonable suspicion is required to strip search arrestees. This suspicion may be based on the conduct of the individual arrestee, and it also may be based on the reason for the arrest. If the person is arrested for a drug-related offense or violent offense, most courts say a strip search at the time of booking is constitutional. A felony charge alone does not necessarily create a cause for a strip search, as shown by two Ninth Circuit cases. In *Kennedy v. Los Angeles Police Department*, the Circuit found that a strip search of a person arrested on a minor property-related felony was not reasonable while only weeks earlier, the same court (but different judges) found that felony auto theft was sufficiently associated with violence to justify a strip search.[10] It may be that a criminal history and/or history of past behavior in the jail could create reasonable suspicion, but this is not clear.

Some jail administrators have argued that when an arrestee is placed in the general population of a jail, a strip search may be conducted. This argument was rejected in the *Kennedy* case—placing the woman arrested for the property offense in the general population did not create justification for a strip search when none existed otherwise. This remains the general rule: where reasonable suspicion did not otherwise exist to strip search an arrestee, placing the person in a general population unit did not allow the person to be strip searched.[11]

In the arrestee strip-search litigation, courts generally define "strip search" broadly, to include any time an arrestee is required to completely disrobe under the observation of a correctional officer. A jail cannot avoid the reasonable suspicion rule by calling the observation a "medical check," or "hygiene check," or "visual observation."[12] A jail that persists in strip searching all arrestees places itself at serious legal risk.

Body-Cavity-Probe Searches

In extreme situations, it may be necessary to physically probe an inmate's body cavities for contraband. Because this is the most intrusive search of the person possible, short of surgery, there must be clear policies and procedures on when, how, and by whom this search is conducted.

In a normal institutional setting, reasonable cause must exist to justify a body-cavity-probe search. There must be some reason to suspect a particular inmate is hiding contraband in a body cavity.[13] In extraordinarily high-security housing units, automatic probe searches, done every time an inmate returns to his or her cell, have been approved, but this is clearly the exception, requiring a very clear showing of the need to justify.[14]

Body-cavity-probe searches are best done only when there is good reason to believe the inmate is carrying contraband in a body cavity (perhaps even probable cause, but certainly reasonable suspicion or belief). The search should be done by medical staff and done in a manner and place that respects the inmate's dignity and privacy as much as is reasonably possible. Facility policy should address circumstances in which body-cavity-probe searches may be done.

Case Study: Body-Cavity-Probe Searches and Court Review

A body-cavity-probe search is as intrusive a search as possible, short of surgery. As such, courts will carefully and critically review the justifications for body-cavity-probe searches as well as the manner in which they are conducted.

The Walla Walla State Penitentiary had a policy of performing digital body-cavity-probe searches, including rectal probes, of every inmate who entered or returned to a super-maximum custody unit. Such a policy was, at best, on the very edge of constitutionality. In an opinion that, for procedural reasons, did not ultimately decide the merits of the case, a reviewing court tentatively decided the searches, as apparently actually carried out, were being done for punitive reasons not related to security concerns. As such, they violated the clearly established rights of the inmates. The court noted the following factors in reaching its conclusion:

1. An officer who picked up one inmate in the general population to escort him to the unit allegedly smiled and said, "Today, you meet Mr. Big Finger."

2. Although every inmate entering the unit was rectally probe-searched, no effort was apparently made to search other body cavities, hair, or even hands. Evidence showed one inmate had smuggled a pack of tobacco into the unit in his pocket.

3. The rectal-probe-search policy allegedly was used by officers as a threat to influence inmates' behavior in the general population.

Tribble v. Gardner, 860 F.2d 321 (9th Cir., 1988).

Visitor Searches

Just as inmates' expectations of privacy are reduced by the fact of incarceration, the expectations of free people entering a correctional facility are reduced, although not as much as inmates. Thus, visitors and staff are more subject to search in the facility than they would be on the street.

Visitors are entitled to greater protections from searches than inmates, although visitors give up some of their expectations of privacy on entering the prison or jail. Routine pat downs, searches of purses and briefcases, and magnetometer searches of all persons entering a facility have been approved. However, courts require reasonable suspicion for a strip search to be performed. Usually even when reasonable suspicion exists, the person may refuse to submit to the search and leave the institution.

A requirement that every visitor "agree" to a strip search as a condition of being allowed to visit jail inmates resulted in an award of $177,000 damages against a Massachusetts sheriff.[15] The court quickly rejected the argument that the visitor "consented" to the searches, saying that at least as a general matter, the state cannot condition the granting of even a privilege (such as visiting) on someone giving up a constitutional right (in this case, the right to be free from unreasonable searches).

Just as reasonable suspicion is required for visitor strip searches, so is it required for staff strip searches. Thus, an anonymous tip did not justify strip searching an officer, since it could not provide reasonable suspicion.[16]

Case Study: Visitor Body-Cavity Probe and Search Warrant

Sometimes even a search warrant does not protect officers from liability for an unconstitutional search. Consider the following case, involving suspected drug trafficking between an inmate and his wife.

Prison officials obtained a search warrant from a local judge allowing them to perform body-cavity searches of an inmate's pregnant wife and infant son. The search was conducted, but no drugs were found. The wife then filed a civil rights action against the prison investigators. Even though the local magistrate had reviewed the affidavit submitted in support of the search warrant and found it adequate, the federal court not only found the affidavit insufficient, but said that "no reasonably competent officer could have believed that the affidavit established probable cause for a body cavity search." Based on this conclusion, the court denied the defendants' qualified immunity, exposing them to liability for damages.

Defendants argued that no probable cause was necessary because the plaintiff was a prison visitor and only reasonable suspicion is required to search prison visitors. Conceding that reasonable suspicion ("specific, objective facts and rational inferences" therefrom) will support a strip search of a visitor, the court found a manual body-cavity-probe search, as was conducted here, to require a search warrant issued upon probable cause. The court found the defendants' argument about reasonable suspicion failed for another reason. When the wife came to the prison and was searched, prison officials were waiting for her, waiting to do the search. They had no intention of allowing her to visit. Since this was the case, the court reasoned that the woman presented no threat to prison security and her search could not be justified as furthering legitimate penological concerns. The situation had changed from one involving prison security to nothing more than a criminal investigation.

Laughter v. Kay, 986 F. Supp. 1362 (D. Utah., 1997).

Observation and Searches by the Opposite Sex

The increased use of women working in male facilities and, to a lesser extent, men working in female facilities, presents a variety of issues, many arising under the Fourth Amendment.

Does it violate the right of privacy of the inmate (which comes in part from the Fourth Amendment) if the inmate is observed taking a shower, using the toilet, or in other states of undress by an officer of the opposite sex? Does it make a difference if the officer is a woman and the inmate male or if the inmate is a woman and the officer male? Can officers search inmates of the opposite sex? If a cross-gender pat-down search is acceptable, is a strip search? Does the guarantee of equal employment opportunity outweigh privacy rights the inmate might have regarding being observed (or touched) by an officer of the opposite sex? Not all of these questions have been answered yet, but some answers are emerging.

Female Officers in Male Units

In *Dothard v. Rawlinson*, the Supreme Court decided that a complete ban on women working in a male prison system did not violate the equal opportunity rights of the women. This decision was not based on inmate privacy concerns, but instead on a concern for the women's safety, in light of the "jungle-like" conditions in the prison.[17] This decision has not been followed by later courts, but instead is limited to its facts. To argue that the *Dothard* case justified an all-male workforce, one virtually would concede conditions in the facility were so unsafe as to be unconstitutional.

The trend now is to hold that when female officers only casually or incidentally observe male inmates in states of undress, it does not violate any rights of the inmates. While some early cases in this area tried to require the institution to accommodate the privacy interests of the inmate through such methods as erecting privacy screens or juggling staff schedules, the trend today is to tolerate limited glimpses of nudity.[18]

This section discusses inappropriate sexual contact between male officers and female inmates and the legal consequences of such inappropriate activity. Note that sexual contact between female officers and male inmates is also a serious problem. A 2008 study by the Bureau of Justice Statistics, *Sexual Victimization in Local Jails Reported by Inmates*, 2007, showed that "nearly 62 percent of all reported incidents of staff sexual misconduct involved female staff with male inmates."[19]

Case Study: Sexual Abuse of Female Inmates

In 2010, one likes to think that correctional agencies run at a high level of professionalism and that the sort of shocking cases which opened the door for court intervention in corrections years ago do not arise anymore. Fortunately, they do not occur with the frequency they once did, but consider the following:

The woman was an inmate in the District of Columbia Jail in 1995. Over the course of a month, correctional officers forced her, along with other female inmates, to participate in strip shows and exotic dances. At least once, the inmates danced in the nude. Several officers were involved, but no supervisory officials apparently knew of the incidents. Eighty to one-hundred women were in the units where the dancing took place, but supervisory officials apparently only became aware of the incidents when the lawsuit was filed.

One inmate testified that she refused to participate and was beaten by an officer. Defendants argued she was beaten for reasons other than refusing to dance. Another inmate testified she participated only out of fear of physical retaliation should she refuse.

Several months prior to the incidents, another federal judge had found there were substantial sexually related problems between male officers and female inmates and ordered remedial steps to be taken. When the incidents took place, all that had been done was the issuance of a new policy and limited training.

Based on these facts, the court directed a verdict in favor of the plaintiff, leaving the jury with only the task of assessing damages. *Newby v. District of Columbia*, 59 F. Supp. 2d 35 (D.D.C. 1999).

Male Officers in Female Facilities

Sexual abuse of female inmates by male officers is a serious problem.[20] This abuse ranges from verbal harassment to unwarranted intrusions upon women's privacy, to unwarranted touching, to physical rape. This conduct may violate the Fourth Amendment, the Eighth Amendment (cruel and unusual punishment), or may be considered criminal behavior, exposing the officer to prosecution. Many states have made any sexual contact between a correctional officer and an inmate a crime. Concerns about sexual abuse of inmates drove Congress to pass the Prison Rape Elimination Act of 2003 (PREA), discussed later in this chapter.

91

In state laws that criminalize sexual contact between staff and inmate, typically, "consent" is not a defense. *Any* sexual contact, regardless of supposed consent, violates the law. Sexual contact between officer and inmate under any circumstances is completely inappropriate, if not illegal. While most of the controversy over officer-inmate sexual contact relates to male officers and female inmates, improper contact between female officers and male inmates also occurs. Undoubtedly, sexual contact between officers and inmates of the same sex also takes place. In all cases, the contact is entirely inappropriate.

In addition to sexual contact, there are also unresolved questions about the extent to which privacy interests of female inmates may justify limiting what male officers can do. Because of concerns over the privacy of female inmates and in restricting sexual contact between male officers and female inmates (or allegations of such contact), the question occasionally arises about whether men can simply be barred from working in female housing units. There are not many cases on this issue, but they all have at least tentatively approved limiting posts that male officers can work in female facilities.

A number of years ago, a court of appeals in the Midwest tentatively approved a ban on men working in female housing units, based on the warden's assertion that removing male officers would enhance the women's rehabilitation because a high percentage of female inmates had previously been physically or sexually abused by men.[21] The case was settled out of court, so the reported decision is not a clear holding that such a ban was valid.

In 1998, the Ninth Circuit approved the Hawaii Department of Corrections' decision to make seven of forty-two posts in the women's prison off limits to male officers.[22] The court found the rule furthered the well-documented interests of the department in protecting the female inmate's privacy interests and in reducing the risk of sexual contact between officers and inmates. The court also noted that not very many jobs there were affected by the decision.

The most dramatic result comes from a case involving a decision of the Michigan Department of Corrections to remove male officers from all female housing unit posts. The decision was initially overturned by the district court but was later approved by the Sixth Circuit Court of Appeals.[23] The court of appeals took pains to say that it was not holding that it was generally approving removing male officers from female housing units but was approving the action in the case before it because of what it described as "endemic" problems of sexual abuse in Michigan's prisons.

The decision also notes the relevance of security concerns that the Michigan Department of Corrections argued were compromised when men worked in female units. These included various privacy accommodations that had been made, including covers for cell windows and a "knock and announce" requirement before male officers could enter an area where female inmates might be undressed. The court also credited testimony saying that there was tension and a "poisoned atmosphere" between male officers and inmates over allegations of sexual misconduct and that the threat of such allegations (whether true or not) made officers "gun-shy" about monitoring inmates properly.

While the district court's decision was reversed, there is a noteworthy statement from that decision. The judge stated explicitly what other court decisions in this area imply: "female inmates being viewed by males is qualitatively different than males being viewed by females."[24] While some argue that if male inmates have few privacy protections vis-a-vis being seen by female officers, then female inmates should have no more privacy expectations when it comes to male officers. Courts do not accept this view and in doing so, they are doing no more than what society as a whole would probably agree on: women have greater privacy concerns about their bodies than do men, particularly when it comes to being seen in states of undress by persons of the opposite sex.

Cross-Gender Pat Searches

Some courts have approved pat searches of male inmates by female officers, while others have done so under the assumption that the searches did not include contact with the genital area.[25] So, it is not totally clear that female officers may pat search male inmates.

While courts may be willing to allow female officers to pat search male inmates, the same cannot be said of male officers pat searching female inmates. This practice has been addressed only once by a federal appeals court, and the court held that the practice was cruel and unusual punishment, in violation of the Eighth Amendment. The court refused to evaluate the searches under the Fourth Amendment. In deciding the searches violated the Eighth Amendment, the court was reacting to expert testimony that said that many of the women, who had been sexually and physically abused prior to coming into prison, would be psychologically traumatized by being pat searched by male officers, since they would see this as a continuation of the abuse they had previously suffered.[26]

In the years following the *Jordan* decision, no other court outside the Ninth Circuit has directly addressed a similar question of male officers pat searching female inmates. *Jordan* did not address the question of female officers pat searching male inmates.

A good deal more litigation will be needed before there are complete, clear answers to the legal questions surrounding cross-gender supervision, although the legal trend at this time seems to continue to favor women working most posts in male facilities. There is greater uncertainty about male officers working in female facilities. Something that makes this area even more difficult to analyze than many other "inmate rights" areas is that it involves conflicts between interests of the inmate and the institution (a common situation) and interests of the officers in equal opportunity and avoiding discrimination.

Where a task requires fairly intensive observation of naked inmates (such as doing strip searches), the task only should be done by persons of the same sex. In emergency situations, considerations of privacy in searches generally are set aside in favor of the institution being able to respond to the emergency in the quickest, safest, most effective way.

Agencies should also not assume that the privacy interests of male and female interests are identical. There is a small, but increasing body of case law that says women have stronger privacy interests than men.

Prison Rape Elimination Act (PREA)

In 2003, Congress passed a statute called the Prison Rape Elimination Act (PREA). Potentially, the most significant part of this law is a requirement that the U.S. Attorney General adopt national standards addressing the prevention of rape in correctional facilities. The standards adoption process has been a very long one, and the final standards are not likely to be adopted before sometime in 2010. PREA also mandated that the Bureau of Justice Statistics (part of the U.S. Department Justice) conduct annual studies about sexual violence in prisons and jails, and these studies, while not perfect, have produced a substantial amount of interesting data about sexual activity in correctional institutions.

The greatest impacts of PREA in the first several years of its existence have been to focus attention on prison rape (including sexual contact between staff and inmates) and to encourage improved training and responses to allegations of sexual misconduct, whether between inmates or between staff and inmates.

Conclusion

The right of inmates to be free from unreasonable searches is drastically less than the right enjoyed by persons outside the institution. However, some protections remain. For the line officer asked to perform searches, the key factors to remember are to follow policy regarding when searches may be performed and to do those searches in a professional manner that respects the dignity of the inmate.

In part because of litigation and in part because of the Prison Rape Elimination Act, the roles of male officers working around female inmates and those of female officers working around male inmates will be undergoing scrutiny and possible change for the next few years.

Review Questions

1. The Supreme Court has held that inmates have no expectation of privacy in regard to their cells. How then might a cell search trigger court intervention?

2. What is necessary to justify visitor strip searches?

3. What is the most important thing for correctional officers to remember when performing inmate searches?

Endnotes

[1] *Bell v. Wolfish*, 441 U.S. 520 (1979).

[2] *Kennedy v. Hardiman*, 684 F.Supp.540 (N.D. Ill., 1980).

[3] *Hudson v. Palmer*, 104 S.Ct. 3194 (1984).

[4] *Block v. Rutherford*, 104 S.Ct. 3227 (1984).

[5] *Bell v. Wolfish*, 441 U.S. 529 (1979).

[6] *Rickman v. Avanti*, 854 F.2d 327 (9th Cir., 1988), *Goff v. Nix*, 803 F.2d 358 (8th Cir., 1986), cert. denied, 108 S.Ct. 115 (1987).

[7] *Covino v. Patrissi*, 967 F.2d 73 (2d Cir., 1992).

[8] In *Chapman v. Nichols*, 989 F.2d 393 (10th Cir., 1993), the court cites opinions from eight different federal appeals courts holding that strip searching arrestees without reasonable suspicion is a violation of the Fourth Amendment. However, see *Powell v. Barrett*, 541 F.3d 1298 (11th Cir., 2008), in which the 11th Circuit rejects a holding from an earlier case and decides no reasonable suspicion is required to strip search all arrestees as part of the booking process.

[9] *Bull v. City and County of San Francisco*, F.3d (2010), *Powell v. Barnett*, 541 F.3d 1298 (11th Cir, 2008).

[10] *Kennedy v. Los Angeles Police Department*, 887 F.2d 920 (9th Cir., 1989), *Thompson v. Los Angeles* (County), 885 F.2d 1439 (9th Cir., 1989).

[11] *Savard v. Rhode Island*, 320 F.3d 34 (1st Cir., 2003).

[12] *Florence v. Board of Chosen Freeholders*, 2009 U.S. Dist. Lexis 7923 (D. N.J. 2009).

13. *Vaughn v. Ricketts*, 663 F.Supp. 410 (D. Ariz., 1987).

14. *Bruscino v. Carlson*, 854 F.3d 162 (7th Cir., 1988).

15. *Blackburn v. Snow*, 771 F.2d 556 (1st Cir., 1985).

16. *Security and Law Enforcement Employees District Council #82 v. Carey*, 737 F.2d 187 (2d Cir., 1984).

17. *Dothard v. Rawlinson*, 433 U.S. 321 (1977).

18. *Michenfelder v. Sumner*, 860 F.2d 328 (9th Cir., 1988). *Hardin v. Stinchomb*, 691 F.2d 1364 (11th Cir., 1982), *Timm v. Gunter*, 917 F.2d 1093 (8th Cir., 1990).

19. *Sexual Victimization in Local Jails Reported by Inmates* 2000, p. 7, Bureau of Justice Statistics, 2008 NCJ 221946.

20. *All Too Familiar: Sexual Abuse of Women in U.S. State Prisons*, Women's Rights Project of Human Rights Watch, New York, 1996.

21. *Torres v. Wisconsin Department of Health and Social Services*, 859 F.2d 1523 (7th Cir., 1988).

22. *Robino v. Iranon*, 145 F.3d 1109 (9th Cir., 1998).

23. *Everson v. Michigan Dept. of Corrections*, 222 F.Supp.2d 864 (E.D.Mich.,2002), rev'd, 391 F.3d 737 (6th Cir., 2004).

24. 222 F. Supp.2d at 896. See also *Colman v. Vasquez*, 142 F.Supp.2d 226 (D.Conn., 2001), where the court makes a similar observation.

25. *Grummett v. Rushen*, 779 F.2d 491 (9th Cir., 1985). Smith v. Fairman, 678 F.2d 52 (7th Cir., 1982).

26. *Jordan v. Gardner*, 986 F.2d 1521 (9th Cir., 1993).

Chapter 8:
The Eighth Amendment: Cruel and Unusual Punishment

The Eighth Amendment addresses bails, fines, and punishments:

> Excessive bail shall not be required, nor excessive fines imposed, nor cruel and unusual punishment inflicted.

Through its "cruel and unusual punishment" clause, the Eighth Amendment has been more significant for corrections than any other amendment during the inmate rights movement. It is through the concept of cruel and unusual punishment that conditions of confinement in a jail, prison, or even an entire prison system may be challenged.

The Eighth Amendment also may provide the legal basis for claims about the use of excess force (*see* Chapter10) as well as the basis for suits challenging such things as the adequacy of medical care or protection afforded an inmate in particular situations. Offenders also may use the Amendment to challenge the length or severity of their sentences (especially in death penalty cases), but this aspect of the amendment is not usually of direct concern to correctional officers, nor are claims relating to excessive bail or fines.

Unlike most other amendments where one may compare what the amendment means, or its scope, between noncustodial situations ("the street") and inside the institution, the Eighth Amendment has no "street" application. Cruel and unusual punishment applies only after an offender has been convicted. Eighth Amendment rights arise or are created by the fact of conviction.

A Vague Concept

The phrase "cruel and unusual punishment" is vague. What may be cruel and unusual punishment to one observer may be standard operating procedure to another. The courts have tried to develop other, clearer ways of defining the concept, but these are also vague phrases that may mean different things to different people. Among the phrases or "tests" the Supreme Court has developed over the years to define or clarify what cruel and unusual punishment means are the following:

- Shocks the conscience of the Court

- Violates the evolving standards of decency of a civilized society

- Punishment that is disproportionate to the offense

- Involves the wanton and unnecessary infliction of pain

Some types of punishment, such as flogging or other forms of physical torture, uniformly would be seen as being cruel and unusual punishment. As with many other conditions and practices, it is not clear whether they are cruel and unusual punishment. Because the concept of cruel and unusual punishment never will have a clear, objective definition that means the same thing to different people, it is virtually impossible to look at every imaginable situation and say with confidence, "This is (or is not) cruel and unusual punishment."

During the early 1990s, the courts seem to have settled on the "wanton and unnecessary infliction of pain" test, with the Supreme Court applying this test in cases involving conditions of confinement and the use of force.[1]

Except for use-of-force claims, Eighth Amendment issues that inmates raise require the court to examine the state of mind of the defendants as part of deciding if the inmate has received cruel and unusual punishment. The defendant must have shown "deliberate indifference" to some significant basic human need of the inmate, such as medical care.

The phrase "deliberate indifference" first appeared in a Supreme Court case in 1976 in the case of *Estelle v. Gamble*.[2] There, the Court said that deliberate indifference to an inmate's serious medical need violated the Eighth Amendment. Deliberate indifference also is relevant in failure-to-protect cases, in conditions-of-confinement cases, and in other cases where an inmate complains that some basic human need is not being met adequately.

Although the concept of deliberate indifference has been part of Eighth Amendment litigation for many years, it was not until 1994 that the Court defined the phrase. In a failure-to-protect case, a transsexual inmate alleged he/she was raped after being placed in the general population of a federal penitentiary. The inmate claimed that officials should have known that placing an effeminate looking and acting individual in the general inmate population placed the person at great risk of sexual assault.

The Court said that to be deliberately indifferent, an official must have actual knowledge that an inmate faces a substantial risk of serious harm and then must disregard that risk by failing to take reasonable steps to abate it.[3] What an official "should have known" cannot be the basis of a deliberate indifference finding. In *Farmer*, it was not clear from the record what the defendants (all at the level of warden or above) actually knew about the inmate's circumstances, so the case was sent back to the lower courts for trial. Ironically, when the case was finally tried, the jury found that the plaintiff failed to prove he even had been sexually assaulted. Therefore, the jury did not have to consider whether the defendants had been deliberately indifferent to the inmate's safety.

Conditions of Confinement

Conditions-of-confinement cases, often referred to as overcrowding cases, have resulted in prisons in almost every state being found unconstitutional at one time or another. As of 2009, at least six states were under court order or consent decrees to limit their prison populations and/or to improve conditions in one or more prisons. In Alabama, Michigan, and Mississippi, the entire prison system was under court order. In Ohio and South Carolina, the entire state was under a consent decree.[4] Hundreds of jails, including the entire New York City system have been under similar orders over the years.[5] Whatever the precise numbers are, large number of America's prisons and jails have been directly affected by conditions-of-confinement lawsuits. Virtually every other facility in the country has been indirectly affected by these suits.

Conditions cases are very complex and may take a long time to prepare for trial. The trial may continue for weeks or even months. However, the time consumed in preparing and trying a conditions case is short compared to the time it often takes to correct problems when a facility is found to violate the Eighth Amendment.

Note: While the Eighth Amendment is the legal vehicle used to attack conditions in prisons, its protections do not apply to persons who have not yet been convicted of a crime. Since *Bell v. Wolfish*, the Due Process Clause of the Fourteenth Amendment is the vehicle used to challenge conditions of pretrial detainees. Despite the differing legal theories used for convicted versus unconvicted persons, the end result for either a prison or a jail, in terms of what conditions are required, is essentially the same.

99

Issues in Conditions Cases

What are the issues in conditions cases? What factors are of concern to the court?

The factors courts have considered in evaluating the conditions of confinement have changed somewhat over the years. Many early cases reacted to the "totality of conditions." Under this approach, virtually all of the negative aspects of a prison would be lumped together for consideration by the court. This could be a very subjective way of analyzing conditions. Along with the totality of conditions approach, courts in the late 1970s began to focus heavily on crowding and a facility's design capacity. Under this method, several courts virtually had reached the point of deciding that if a facility held more inmates than it was designed to hold, it was in an unconstitutional state.

The Supreme Court first addressed conditions of confinement in the case of *Bell v. Wolfish*, where it held that there was "no one-man, one-cell principle lurking" in the Constitution, at least as far as pretrial detainees were concerned. *Bell* said that the effects of crowding on the inmates, not simply the fact of crowding, were what courts should evaluate in conditions cases. The Court reemphasized this point two years later in a case that dealt with sentenced offenders, *Rhodes v. Chapman*.[6] Conditions that are restrictive, or even harsh, do not violate the Eighth Amendment, said Justice Powell in his majority opinion. Only when conditions "deprive inmates of the minimal civilized measure of life's necessities" do they violate the Constitution, said the Court. *Bell and Rhodes* ended any thought that a crowded institution was per se unconstitutional.

Ten years passed before the Supreme Court again decided a conditions-of-confinement case. In *Wilson v. Seiter*,[7] the court added a new factor that must be shown in order for an institution to violate the Eighth Amendment: the inmates must prove the defendants (the persons responsible for operating the institution) were "deliberately indifferent" to conditions that denied inmates "the minimal civilized measure of life's necessities."

So, after *Wilson*, there are two separate factors that must be shown. Unless the plaintiffs (the inmates) prove both of these factors, they cannot win their case. The factors are as follows:

1. The conditions must be very bad, creating a substantial risk of serious harm by failing to adequately provide inmates with one or more basic human need, and

2. The defendants knew of the serious problems and failed to take any sort of meaningful corrective response (deliberate indifference).

The *Wilson* decision also said that a totality-of-conditions approach was incorrect. Different conditions (such as poor medical care, poor sanitation, high levels of violence) must be considered separately from one another except "when they have a mutually enforcing effect that produces the deprivation of a single, identifiable human need such as food, warmth, or exercise—for example, a low cell temperature at night combined with a failure to issue blankets."

The conditions that are the focus of the first part of the *Wilson* test will be ones that deal with the basic human needs of the inmates, including:

1. **Food.** Do inmates receive a nutritionally adequate diet, and is food prepared and served in an acceptably sanitary manner?

2. **Clothing.** Does inmate clothing provide adequate protection given the climatic conditions, and does it provide adequate privacy protections for the inmates (is it full of holes, ragged, and so forth)? Clothing is rarely a significant issue in conditions cases anymore.

3. **Shelter.** This category looks at the overall environment of the institution, including such things as noise levels; heating; cooling; ventilation; lighting; plumbing; water supplies; overall conditions of the building; maintenance; cell size; exercise and other activity areas and opportunities, and so forth. Shelter issues often arise in cases involving old facilities.

4. **Sanitation.** This relates closely to both food and shelter. Does the plumbing leak badly? Is the institution infested with vermin? Is the facility dirty? Are proper food preparation and handling practices followed? In short, is sanitation so bad as to be a threat to the health of the inmates? While many problems in a conditions case may be beyond the power of the line officer, sanitation is one area where institution staff can do a lot simply by insisting that the inmates keep their living units and activity areas clean and making sure that sufficient cleaning supplies are available to allow this to be done.

5. **Medical care.** Medical care is often the subject of a separate lawsuit that focuses just on the medical service delivery system. The question will be whether the medical system is so deficient as to show "deliberate indifference to the serious medical needs" of the inmates.

While issues in the medical area can become quite complex and technical, the fundamental questions in evaluating the adequacy of a medical system are these: Can inmates (1) get prompt, timely access to properly trained and qualified medical professionals, (2) receive generally appropriate diagnosis of medical problems, and (3) receive timely and appropriate treatment at least for "serious" medical needs? "Medical care" includes dental and mental health care.

6. **Personal safety.** Are inmates reasonably safe in the institution, or is there a serious risk of assault, rape, or other serious injury from other inmates? The adequacy of classification systems often is at issue here: Does the facility have a functional way of separating types of inmates from one another so as to provide adequate protection? In evaluating safety issues, a court often will look at such things as violence levels and rates and requests for protective custody. Personal safety (or, if seen from the other side of the issue, violence levels in the institution) is often the most serious issue in crowding cases, where the sheer number of inmates may make it virtually impossible to maintain an adequate level of safety.

7. **Exercise.** In relatively extreme situations, the lack of exercise may amount to cruel and unusual punishment. Lack of exercise generally only becomes an issue in maximum-security units where inmates may be locked down without any exercise for extended periods of time.

Crowding is not a direct concern of the court in deciding whether conditions in an institution violate the Constitution. At the same time, crowding is probably now the single most important factor in conditions cases, because as a facility becomes more and more crowded, the systems it has in place to provide basic human needs to inmates become overloaded and break down. For instance, crowding can overload the classification system, resulting in inmates not being properly separated from one another, and, in turn, contributing to an increase in violence in the institution. Other factors that also are important include the age and physical condition of the institution, the training and supervision of the officers, and the overall quality of management.

While a court cannot hold a facility unconstitutional simply because it is crowded, if the court decides that crowding was a primary cause of the facility's unconstitutionality, (such as having excessively high levels of violence), crowding can become a focus of a relief order. The court's power to impose population caps or population-reduction orders was limited by Congress in 1996 with the passage of the Prison Litigation Reform Act (PLRA). Under the PLRA, only a three-judge federal court can enter an order imposing population restrictions on an institution and such an order cannot be imposed unless other, less restrictive orders have been tried and failed. As this is written in 2010, California is the only state in which a PLRA population reduction order has been entered. California is still challenging the validity of the order.

Most conditions/crowding cases examine circumstances in an entire institution. However, sometimes the cases are more focused, and scrutinize conditions in specialized living units such as segregation, protective custody, or death row. The basic factual and legal questions in such cases are the same as in a "normal" conditions case.

Relief in Conditions Cases

Lawsuits for damages may be effectively over shortly after trial (or appeal). If damages are awarded and paid, the case is over. However, conditions cases typically do not ask for damages. They ask the court to order the defendants to correct the problems that caused the facility to be unconstitutional. If the court enters such an order (an *injunction*) or if the defendants agree to such an order being entered against them (a *consent decree*), the court will continue to monitor what the defendants do until the institution or system complies with the order. This is known as the *relief phase* of the suit.

Since conditions in many facilities may be very poor or the relief requirements so complex, it often has taken years for the defendants to improve conditions to the point where the court will agree that the case may be closed. It is not uncommon for conditions cases to remain open and active for ten-to-fifteen years. For example, the entire Texas Department of Criminal Justitice came under court order in a massive conditions case in 1978, at a time when the Department consisted of nearly thirty institutions and about 40,000 inmates. Defendants attempted to have the case dismissed in 1999 under the Prison Litigation Reform Act. The court grudgingly found that parts of the system met minimum constitutional requirements but that others did not, so the motion to terminate was granted in part and denied in part. Finally, on June 4, 2002, nearly a quarter century after it was filed, the case was dismissed. Had it not been for the Prison Litigation Reform Act making it easier for such cases to be dismissed, the case would undoubtedly be pending still. As institution populations surge, a facility trying to work itself out from under a court order based largely on crowding problems may find itself going backward, as the population continues to grow faster than inmates can be released or new facilities constructed to hold them.

The Courts' Traditional Approach to Relief

Historically, it was not the court decisions finding that conditions violated the Eighth Amendment, which created the controversy about court intervention in the operation of prisons or jails. The source of the controversy usually arose over what the court ordered defendants to do to correct the problems that created the constitutional violations. The effects of the relief a court ordered could extend from the institution, which was the subject of the lawsuit, to an entire department, and to an entire criminal justice system. For instance, the population cap imposed in the Texas case (referred to earlier) caused serious crowding problems (and related lawsuits) in jails across Texas because the Department could not accept convicted felons from local jails as fast as needed. Struggling with a population cap in a local jail could affect police arrest practices, charging policies of prosecutors, and judges' decisions regarding bail and sentencing.

Where a court order addressed operational conditions (as opposed to just population levels), it became common for courts to appoint persons to oversee compliance, with a very detailed court order. (Defendants often settled cases through consent decrees in which the defendants voluntarily agreed to comply with rigid, detailed requirements and further agreed to the appointment of a monitor.) These persons were given different titles, different responsibilities, and differing levels of power over the defendants. The generic term used to describe them is *special master*.

Traditionally, the court's relief power in this type of case is broad and very strong. While court orders typically would begin in a way the court felt was minimally intrusive, the court had the power to require defendants to address all of the underlying causes of constitutional problems. Therefore, in cases where the problems were very complex, and/or where the defendants did not appear capable of correcting problems without very active oversight, the court might enter a much more detailed, demanding order. In cases where problems appeared to be the result of crowding, these orders often took the form of population caps.

In rare, extreme situations, judges have ordered facilities closed when constitutional violations were very serious and apparently never-ending.[8] In addition to entering more demanding court orders in response to defendants' continuing failure to correct constitutional problems, courts also have exercised their traditional contempt of court powers and imposed fines on defendants. In a long-running case involving prison conditions in Puerto Rico, fines imposed on defendants (and actually paid) exceeded 200 million dollars! And as the twenty-first century moves onward, the case seems likely to continue for several years to come.[9]

Case Study: Failure to Keep Promises Contributes to Big Contempt Fine

By agreement in 1982, the defendants agreed to the entry of a consent decree, which included a 594-inmate cap on the jail and other commitments about conditions in the jail. Six years later, the cap still had not been met. A second consent decree was entered into in 1987, agreeing to essentially the same things, but on a different schedule. A third agreement was entered in 1988, which included a provision for fining the defendants $100 per day per inmate over the cap if the cap were not met.

The defendants failed to meet the time limits in the decrees, even though they had agreed to them. Various hearings were held, all showing the defendants' noncompliance. After hearings in 1989, the district court imposed fines totaling more than $3.4 million, a figure that was actually reduced from what two court masters recommended. The court also ordered that the fine monies be used in part for a bail fund.

Among other comments, the judge noted ". . . the County defendants . . . have not yet spent a single dime towards alleviating the critical housing problem. [The County defendants] made the promises; they did not keep them." *Essex County Jail Inmates v. Amato*, 726 F. Supp. 539 (D. N.J., 1989).

Note: This decision was from 1989. The case did not end until 2005!

A court usually would retain jurisdiction over a facility found unconstitutional until the requirements of the court's orders were met and it appeared that circumstances were such that if the court relinquished its oversight, the problems were not likely to return. Especially in consent decrees, where defendants had agreed in fact to do more than the Constitution might actually require, the court would continue its oversight until the requirements of the decree were met.

Case Study: Harsh Conditions Not Unconstitutional for Worst of the Bad

Denying an inmate outdoor exercise for most of five years, forcing him to shower in restraints, removing his clothing at times, feeding him "nutraloaf" instead of a regular diet, placing him in constantly lit "quiet cells" are cruel and unusual punishment in some situations, perhaps, but not in the case of an inmate named Samuel LeMaire.

Mr. LeMaire was the worst of the bad in the Oregon State Prison system. Serving a "life without possibility of parole" sentence, he built up what the court called an "egregious" record of the most serious types of rule violations. He attacked a sergeant and later threatened to kill him. He stabbed an inmate he thought was a snitch. He tried to stab two other officers. He routinely threw feces and urine on officers. As a result of his behavior, Mr. LeMaire spent most of five years in segregation where officials imposed the conditions he complained of from time to time. The officials carefully documented Mr. LeMaire's behavior and their attempts to respond to it in less dramatic ways. There was nothing in the record to suggest officials acted unprofessionally toward Mr. LeMaire, despite obvious provocation.

The court of appeals said that Mr. LeMaire was "the master of his own fate" and that the officials were justified in taking the steps they did. Given the extraordinary nature of Mr. LeMaire's actions, the court said that only if the record showed officials to be acting maliciously and sadistically, rather than attempting to maintain order, security, and discipline, would they violate Mr. LeMaire's rights. *LeMaire v. Maass*, 12 F.3d 1444 (9th Cir., 1993).

In other circumstances, a court might have intervened in response to these sorts of conditions. However, the documentation by Oregon officials demonstrated the appropriateness of their actions.

The Prison Litigation Reform Act and Relief

In passing the Prison Litigation Reform Act in 1996, Congress attempted to check the power of the federal courts in conditions cases. The Act begins by reinforcing the principle that injunctions in prison cases should go no further than is minimally necessary to correct constitutional violations. The most dramatic aspect of this part of the statute is the limitation on when population caps or reduction orders can be issued. These limitations were discussed earlier in this chapter.

Terminating injunctive orders becomes much easier under PLRA. Two years after such an order is entered, defendants may ask that it be terminated. This motion must be granted unless the court finds that some form of continuing injunctive order is needed to correct a continuing violation of a federal right. In other words, there virtually may have to be a new trial to justify continuing relief.

Special provisions exist for terminating existing consent decrees and other injunctive orders. The law tries to make the very detailed consent decree, which often includes requirements beyond minimal demands of the Constitution, virtually impossible.

The powers of special masters are restricted to assisting in the development of remedial plans, holding hearings, and making proposed findings of fact. Levels of compensation for masters are fixed in the Act and now must be paid by the federal court. Defendants no longer may be required to pay costs related to a master, which in some cases in the past have amounted to hundreds of thousands of dollars.

While PLRA attempted to limit the powers of "special masters," courts still have authority to appoint monitors and take other extraordinary steps to bring about compliance with court orders. In a very extreme situation, a California federal judge in 2006 appointed an official called a "receiver" with the power to literally take over complete control of the inmate medical system in California's huge prison system. The Department did not oppose appointment of this official. The powers given the receiver are staggering. He can exercise all of the powers normally vested in the head of the corrections department regarding operation of the medical system; he can hire and fire state employees, create or abolish staff positions, and acquire property and equipment. The state is required to pay the costs associated with the receiver carrying out his duties, which in 2008 were projected to run into billions of dollars for new facilities and staff.

How did this come about? California's medical system had been under court orders for a number of years and the department was unable to comply with the requirements of those orders, many of which the Department had agreed to. The judge presiding over the case felt that without taking the extraordinary step of appointing a receiver, improvements to the medical system might never come.

All major provisions of the PLRA have survived constitutional attack.

The Supreme Court's decision in *Lewis v. Casey*[10] strongly affirmed the High Court's belief that lower courts should proceed conservatively in ordering relief.

Alternatives to Lawsuits?

Conditions of confinement lawsuits have generated a great deal of controversy. Administrators have chafed at what they perceived (rightly so, in at least some cases) as excessive oversight from courts and masters. State and local politicians have complained about unelected federal officials in effect setting spending and criminal justice policy priorities for them. Some members of the public believe courts are responsible for creating "country club" prisons.

However, court intervention usually begins for a reason: an institution has very serious operational problems, perhaps the result of crowding, perhaps the result of other causes, including lack of funding or poor management. The problems are creating serious threats to the health or safety of inmates (and staff, although this is not an issue in the cases). Crowding may be so bad that inmates are sleeping on the floors of cells with their head almost under the toilet. Staff largely may have abandoned any efforts to keep inmates safe from one another. Where court intervention is most dramatic, one often will find that officials have failed to correct problems, which a court has found violate the rights of the inmates. The scope of the intervention has grown largely in proportion to officials' inability or refusal to address major problems seriously.

Defendants in many cases, while grumbling at times about court oversight, also will admit that without the lawsuit and without the court's orders, necessary improvements never would have been made. Instead, problems would have continued to get worse, increasing risks to both staff and inmates alike. Correctional officials may have been trying to address problems but lacked the power and the resources to solve them. Wardens and jail commanders do not determine how long inmates stay in custody. They do not appropriate the funds to increase staffing, or improve medical care. It may be that only through litigation and court intervention that the officials who do hold the keys and the purse strings can be made to focus attention on correcting very serious deficiencies. Therefore, as controversial as court intervention sometimes may be, in many cases, a lawsuit or the serious threat of one may be the only effective protection against conditions deteriorating to truly unacceptable levels.

More than one correctional administrator has chosen not to invoke the provisions of the Prison Litigation Reform Act, which would allow termination of existing court orders or consent decrees because of the protections the court order provides.

Individual Eighth Amendment Issues

Eighth Amendment claims involving conditions of confinement and many inmates in a class action suit draw a great deal of attention. However, Eighth Amendment issues also can arise around a single inmate. Virtually any of the issues, which can be raised in a class action Eighth Amendment case, can be asserted by one inmate. Two types of these issues deserve special comment: medical care and failure to protect.

Medical Care

Where medical care (or the lack thereof) shows "deliberate indifference to serious medical needs," an Eighth Amendment violation exists. Medical staff can violate the Eighth Amendment. In one case, an inmate lost a large portion of his ear in a fight. He asked the doctor to sew the ear back on, but the doctor's response was to refuse the request and throw the ear in a wastebasket as the inmate watched.[11] This illustrates deliberate indifference to a serious medical need.

Other refusals by medical staff to treat inmates can create liability. The refusal by a physician's assistant to approve an X-ray for an inmate complaining of a hip injury after jumping off a truck led to a $500,000 judgment when the inmate—after only a few months in jail—had to have a total hip replacement as a result of the refusal to make any serious attempt to diagnose and treat the inmate's complaints. (The physician's assistant even refused an offer from the inmate's mother to pay for the X-ray.)[12]

Nonmedical staff also can violate the Eighth Amendment in the medical area when they impede an inmate's access to medical staff or the inmate's access to treatment, once it has been prescribed. This could involve custody staff refusing to process an inmate's request to see medical staff or refusing to allow the inmate to have crutches prescribed by a doctor because they were seen as a security threat.

Security concerns sometimes conflict with medical needs. Ignoring medical concerns for security reasons often can lead to liability. The following example is typical. An inmate is seen for an arm injury by institution medical staff, who decide the inmate needs to be transported to a local hospital for additional treatment. The doctor orders the inmate to be transported and that the inmate's arm be kept elevated during the transport. Without checking with anyone in the medical department, the transportation lieutenant overrides the "arm elevated" order because institution policy says all inmates transported outside the institution must be put in shackles and waist chains. The lieutenant's decision probably would be seen as "deliberate indifference." If the arm injury were serious and aggravated by not being kept elevated, the lieutenant could be liable.

Failure to respond to medical emergencies can create liability. Jail staff left a sixty-two-year-old in a living area where temperatures reached 110 degrees with no ventilation and extraordinarily high humidity, even though a nurse had recommended the inmate be moved. The sheriff had warned that people could die in the heat, but the county commission had done nothing to relieve the conditions because of a lack of money. There was not even a fan in the unit. The inmate passed out and, although jail staff were immediately aware of this, the inmate was given no first aid and was not taken to an emergency room for two hours. Diagnosed as suffering from heatstroke, the inmate died a few days later.[13]

The conditions in the cell, known to the sheriff and the county commission, were found to be cruel and unusual. A lack of any medical treatment from the officers showed deliberate indifference. These factors, combined with the inadequate emergency response, led to a $100,000 compensatory damage award to the victim's children and a $10,000 punitive damage award. An attorneys' fees award, probably approaching the size of the damage award, also was given. Despite all of the other heat problems, had there been a prompt emergency response that saved the inmate's life, the suit might never have been brought. Certainly, the damages would have been far lower. This case provides an example of how "rights" to things that seem like luxuries may develop. In this case, it was a right to air temperatures that did not threaten the health of inmates that translates into air conditioning. Looked at in isolation, the "right to air conditioning" seems extreme. However, suppose the case had asked for some sort of injunctive relief, instead of just asking for damages.

The court finds that the defendants were deliberately indifferent to the health needs of at least one inmate, and perhaps all the inmates, because they did nothing to relieve the extreme temperature and humidity conditions that caused one inmate to suffer a heatstroke. Having found the temperature and humidity conditions to be unconstitutional, the court asks itself: "What relief should we order that would cure this constitutional problem (excessive, health-threatening heat and humidity in the jail)?" One obvious answer is air conditioning. So, the court enters an order requiring the jail to provide air conditioning. Other persons read this order and begin to decide air conditioning must be required in jails. Other cases, also reacting to the facts, order air conditioning, and soon the "right to air conditioning" has become well established. On closer examination, the right may not be to air conditioning, but instead to "temperatures that are not so high or so low as to endanger the health of the inmates." Yet, in some climates, the only way this can be done is through air conditioning.

A common potential problem with medical care arises late at night, when an inmate suddenly says he or she needs to see a doctor. The custody staff member who tells that inmate to "wait until sick call tomorrow" is making a medical decision that whatever ailment the inmate has is not serious enough to warrant immediate attention. Should a serious medical problem develop before sick call (such as appendicitis), the custody staff member could be liable. If the "wait until tomorrow" response is proper under agency policy, the agency also would be liable. Correctional facilities should develop a means by which the late-night call for medical attention can be responded to by medical staff (even if by telephone), not left to the judgment of custody staff who are not trained to make medical decisions.

Case Study: Ignoring Doctor's Orders

The inmate returned from an outside hospital where emergency surgery had been performed on the inmate's finger. (The emergency developed because of poor care the inmate received from the prison medical staff, but that is not the point of this discussion.) The inmate alleged that the surgeon prescribed a narcotic pain reliever to be given to the inmate as needed. The inmate repeatedly asked the prison doctor and nurse for the medication, but they refused to give it to him. The nurse was quoted as saying "You will get pain medication when I want you to have it, and I don't want you to have it." The doctor told the inmate that he wouldn't give him any medication because the inmate just wanted to get high.

Based on these facts, the court found the inmate had a serious medical need, and the nurse and the prison doctor refused to address that need by refusing the pain medication. If the inmate could prove his allegations, the nurse and the doctor would be deliberately indifferent. If the nurse and doctor could show at trial that the inmate was not in pain but was, in fact, malingering and trying to get the narcotic in order to get high, then their actions would be justified. *Walker v. Benjamin*, 293 F.3d 1030 (7th Cir., 2002).

HIV/AIDS

There is no doubt that AIDS is a serious medical condition requiring appropriate medical treatment. Sometimes correctional staff may have to move rapidly to provide treatment for an inmate with AIDS. For example, a man who was in the final stages of AIDS was arrested on a bench warrant. He told jail staff during the booking process that he was taking the "AIDS cocktail" of drugs for his disease. Although jail medical staff, including the booking nurse, knew that if the medication regimen the arrestee was on were not strictly followed, the medications could lose their effectiveness. The man did not receive any medications for between forty-eight and seventy-two hours. The jail's pharmacy did not maintain the drugs, and it took the booking nurse two days to contact the doctor to obtain permission to have the man's family bring his medications to the jail. The man produced evidence that his viral load soared as a result of not getting the drugs. Based on these facts, the court of appeals reversed a summary judgment granted to the defendants, saying there were material facts at issue regarding possible deliberate indifference by medical staff around the delay and about the possible injury the inmate sustained because of the delay.[14]

Segregation of HIV positive inmates. For a time, some states segregated HIV-positive inmates from the remainder of the prison population. Alabama's policy of complete segregation survived a major legal challenge in the early 1990s, but subsequently, the state has largely abandoned the segregation policy.[15] The Alabama decision said it was permissible under the Constitution to segregate HIV-positive inmates. However, courts have consistently refused to find officials to be deliberately indifferent for not segregating HIV-positive inmates, for not instituting wholesale AIDS testing or for allowing HIV-positive inmates to work in a kitchen and use the same utensils as other inmates.[16]

Access to Medical Records and Information

Inmate medical records and personal medical information is considered confidential and off-limits to nonmedical staff, except in limited circumstances.[17] However, the question of whether inmates have a constitutional right to privacy with regard to their medical records and information is still one about which courts differ. This is not an Eighth Amendment issue, but it fits in a discussion about medical care. The Second and Third Circuits agree that there is a constitutionally based privacy protection for inmate medical records and information but that the right may be curtailed for legitimate penological interests under the traditional four-part *Turner* test (*see* Chapter 5).[18] However, the Sixth Circuit, in a somewhat older decision, rejected the argument that an inmate had any privacy interests that protected disclosure of his HIV status.[19]

A question that correctional officers have raised over the years is whether they should be told which inmates are HIV-positive. Courts have not addressed this question directly and the limited case law that comes close to addressing the question is ambivalent. The argument that officers should know such information is weakened by several practical factors. The institution is not likely to know which inmates are HIV-positive, particularly in a jail where there is a high turnover among inmates. The more officers who know such information, the more likely it will leak out to other inmates. By following universal precautions and treating all bodily fluids as potentially hazardous, this virtually eliminates a broad need to know.

The *Delie* case[20] involved alleged disclosures of an inmate's HIV status through three different means. The inmate alleged that medical staff told officers escorting him to sick call of his medical condition, that the door to clinic exam rooms was left open so both staff and inmates in the waiting room could hear discussions between the inmate and his doctor, and finally that nurses calling him up for medications would announce medications he was being called up for loudly enough for others in the area to hear.

The lower court dismissed the case for failing to state a claim, meaning that the prison officials had not had to provide any information to support their practices (assuming the plaintiff's allegations were accurate). Because the court of appeals disagreed with the lower court's conclusion that inmates had no right to privacy regarding medical information, the case normally would have been sent back to the lower court to allow it to hear from officials and to apply the *Turner* test to whatever information the officials provided.

However, the court of appeals felt this was not necessary because it decided the right to privacy was not clearly established before its decision and, therefore, the officials were entitled to qualified immunity protection against the inmate's claim for damages. Since the inmate had not asked for injunctive relief, the successful qualified immunity defense effectively ended the case. Had the case been decided otherwise, we do not know what justifications the officials might have offered nor how the court might have responded to them.

Case Study: Don't Die on My Shift

It was a cold, snowy night outside a Colorado prison. An inmate began to experience chest pains and other symptoms of a heart attack. His cell partner called the officer who in turn called the lieutenant. The symptoms the inmate described were signs a lay person would recognize. The lieutenant had the authority to order the inmate transported to a hospital but did not do so because of the snow and the time necessary to warm up the van. He allegedly told the inmate "just don't die on my shift. It's too much paper work."

Knowledge of a serious medical need plus a failure to respond equals deliberate indifference. The "don't die on my shift" remark accentuated the lieutenant's state of mind. *Sealock v. Colorado*, 218 F.3d 1205 (10th Cir., 2000).

However, a 2003 decision from the Seventh Circuit dealt with facts somewhat similar to those in *Delie,* and concluded that allowing correctional officers to sit in the exam room where they could easily overhear conversations between an inmate-patient and his treating physician was acceptable under the *Turner* test—at least when the inmate is housed in a very high-security prison. The inmate in this case was not complaining about disclosure of information as sensitive as HIV status but rather what the court described as "pedestrian maladies."[21]

While the district court decision had approved the practice of allowing the officers in exam rooms as a generally reasonable security measure, the court of appeals' decision is much more limited, concluding only that the practice did not violate any of the plaintiff's rights. It noted that it "reserve[d] for another day a fuller treatment of" the question of inmates' right to privacy in the medical context. So, courts have yet to clearly address the question of whether an inmate's HIV status could be disclosed to all officers as a general matter.

Smoking

Prisons and jails have not been immune from the public controversy around smoking and exposure to secondhand smoke. Whereas not so many years ago, correctional agencies might defend their policies of providing free tobacco products to inmates, now the issue is more likely to be whether the institution can go smoke-free or even whether it must provide a smoke-free environment.

Courts have denied inmate claims that they had a constitutionally protected right to smoke, thus approving smoke-free institutions.[22] In 2010, thirty-four states had instituted a smoking ban. Numerous jails around the country, from very small through huge, mega-jail systems, have stopped all smoking. Contrary to fears that going smoke-free would provoke disturbances, most report the transition went smoothly and that the result is a substantial improvement. Among other benefits (including lower health-care costs) is a reduction in the number of fires inmates set, since they no longer have any reason for having matches. Some jail administrators note that perhaps their main problem with the smoke-free facility is officers smuggling cigarettes to inmates.

In mid-1993, the Supreme Court decided that under extreme circumstances, exposing an inmate to secondhand cigarette smoke could violate the Eighth Amendment by posing an "unreasonable risk of serious damage to (the inmate's) future health."[23] The court clearly did not say that inmates have a right to a smoke-free environment. Only if the inmate could show the exposure was so serious as to create a risk that is "one that today's society chooses not to tolerate" and that prison officials were deliberately indifferent to the condition would an Eighth Amendment violation be proven. Meeting the burden of the *Helling* case has proven difficult, and courts clearly are not requiring smoke-free institutions.[24]

The type of smoking case with the greatest chance of inmate success is one where the inmate has a pre-existing medical condition, such as asthma, that is worsened by exposure to secondhand smoke yet continues to be exposed to smoke in his living unit. A Virginia inmate raised such concerns after being double-celled with an inmate who smoked. The complaining inmate said that he had a respiratory problem and could not tolerate tobacco smoke. The inmate asked for help from housing officers, medical staff, and grievance staff, all to no avail. Indeed, the responses to his complaints generally ignored the merits of the complaints, in other words, that exposure to tobacco smoke made the inmate sick. The court said that the plaintiff's allegations stated a claim for relief and that defendants were not entitled to qualified immunity.[25]

The Supreme Court's smoking case is more important for addressing when risk of harm might violate the Eighth Amendment than for its specifics regarding smoking. The general principle that the case recognizes is that where there is an unreasonable risk of serious harm to inmates coming from a condition in the institution, the Eighth Amendment may be violated. Stated bluntly, this means that prison officials cannot expect to defend poor conditions or practices by arguing that "nobody is dead yet" as a result of the conditions.

Tort Suits

In addition to violating the Eighth Amendment, inadequate medical care also can be the basis of a tort suit, in which it would be alleged that the care given was negligent. These cases would be brought in state court, not federal court. Showing "deliberate indifference" is legally more difficult than showing mere negligence, so tort actions about medical care may be easier for the inmate to win than civil rights suits alleging a violation of the Eighth Amendment.

Failure to Protect

While the institution does not guarantee an inmate's safety, deliberate indifference to the inmate's safety violates the Eighth Amendment. (Negligently failing to protect the inmate also may be a tort.) So, while the institution does not guarantee an inmate's safety, the institution staff do have a duty to protect inmates from one another and to maintain generally acceptable levels of safety. As with medical suits, failure-to-protect suits can challenge either actions (or failures to take actions) by individual officers or can challenge the safety in an entire facility.

An Eighth Amendment violation was found under the following facts, which led the jury to award both compensatory and punitive damages to the inmate: An inmate asked not to be put in the general population in the prison after coming to the institution from administrative segregation in a local jail. The request was denied. Later, a knife was found in the inmate's cell. He claimed it was "for protection" and again requested protective custody. The request was denied. Two months later, the inmate was assaulted and again asked to be removed from his cell mate. The request was denied. The cell partner later instigated a fight between the inmate and another inmate. The cell partner testified that he told a staff member to get the inmate off the floor (out of the unit). An officer with authority to move the inmate was shown to be aware of these requests and warnings. The officer was liable.[26]

Facilitywide failure-to-protect suits are one of the most common byproducts of serious crowding, where simply the number of inmates (perhaps combined with the limited number of staff) makes adequate classification and supervision of inmates impossible.

Case Study: Institution Does Not Guarantee Safety

An inmate was stabbed by two other inmates. The victim filed a suit against several institution officials. The evidence showed that in the weeks preceding the stabbing, officials had received two anonymous calls saying the plaintiff was in danger. In each case, officials had spoken to the inmate, who told them he knew of nothing unusual. Therefore, he was not placed in protective custody, but instead remained in the general population. Were the officials liable for a failure to protect? No. The court said that under a "deliberate indifference" standard, it was not enough to show officials were negligent. The evidence must show officials acted recklessly, that they disregarded a substantial, known risk, and that there was a strong likelihood, not simply a possibility, of injury to the inmate. Under the facts here, no such recklessness was shown. *Lewis El v. O'Leary*, 631 F. Supp. 60 (N.D. Ill., 1986).

Conclusion

While court involvement in corrections may be diminishing in many areas, even some areas protected by the Eighth Amendment, court involvement remains active in conditions–of-confinement cases as the number of incarcerated inmates in America continues to soar. In contrast to other areas of law, the fundamental legal tests that govern conditions of confinement have not been significantly changed since the early 1980s. The Eighth Amendment is the source of the greatest court influence in corrections and is likely to remain so for the indefinite future.

Review Questions

1. Who should make the decision on whether an inmate needs medical care?

2. What are the general areas a court will focus on in a conditions-of-confinement suit?

3. Why is crowding an important issue in conditions suits?

Endnotes

1. *Wilson v. Seiter*, 501 U.S. 294 (1991), conditions; *Hudson v. McMillian*, 112 S.Ct. 995 (1992), use of force.

2. *Estelle v. Gamble,* 429 U.S. 97 (1976).

3. *Farmer v. Brennan*, 114 S.Ct. 1970 (1944).

4. American Correctional Association. 2009. *Juvenile and Adult Correctional Departments, Institutions, Agencies and Paroling Authorities Directory.* Alexandria, Virginia: American Correctional Association.

5. "Adult Court Orders and Consent Decrees, Year 2008" in American Correctional Association, 2009 *Directory of Adult Correctional Departments, Institutions, Agencies, and Probation and Parole Authorities,* Alexandria, Virginia: American Correctional Association.

6. *Rhodes v. Chapman*, 101 S.Ct. 2392 (1981).

7. *Wilson v. Seiter*, 111 S.Ct. 2321 (1991).

8. *Morales-Feliciano v. Parole Board of the Commonwealth of Puerto Rico,* 887 F.2d 1 (1st Cir., 1989), *Ahrens v. Thomas,* 434 F.Supp. 873 (W.D. Mo., 1977).

9. *Morales-Feliciano v. Hernandez Colon,* 775 F.Supp. 487 (D. Puerto Rico, 1991).

10. *Lewis v. Casey*, 518 U.S. 343 (1996). See Ch. 4 for additional discussion of the *Lewis* case, which dealt both with lower courts' relief powers and inmates' right of access to the courts.

11. *Williams v. Vincent*, 508 F.2d 541 (2d Cir., 1974).

12. *Mandel v. Doe*, 888 F.2d 783 (11th Cir., 1989).

13. *Brock v. Warren County*, 713 F.Supp. 238 (E.D. Tenn., 1989).

14. *Sullivan v. County of Pierce*, 2000 U.S. App. LEXIS 8254 (9th Cir., 2000).

15. *Harris v. Thigpen*, 941 F.3d 1495 (11th Circuit, 1991).

16. *Robbins v. Clarke*, 946 F.2d 1331 (8th Cir. 1991), *Glick v. Henderson*, 855 F.2d 536 (8th Cir. 1988), *Portee v. Tollison*, 753 F. Supp. 184 (D.S.C. 1990).

17. American Correctional Association's *Adult Correctional Institution* Standard 4-4396 recognizes that medical records and information about an offender's health are confidential but also disclosure may be necessary. However, in these cases, "[o]nly the information necessary to preserve the health and safety of an offender, other offenders, volunteers/visitors, or the correctional staff is provided." See the American Correctional Association's *2010 Standards Supplement* for the latest iteration of this standard.

18. *Doe v. Delie*, 257 F.3d 309 (3rd Cir.,2001), *Powell v. Schriver*, 175 F.3d 107, 112 n.3 (2d Cir. 1999).

19. *Doe v. Wigginton*, 21 F.3d 733 (6th Cir., 1994).

20. *Doe v. Delie*, 257 F.3d 309 (3rd Cir.,2001).

21. *Franklin v. McCaughtry*, 110 Fed. Appx. 715, 720 (7th Cir. Wis. 2004).

22. *Grass v. Sargent*, 903 F.2d 1207 (8th Cir., 1990), *Doughty v. Board of County Commissioners for County of Weld*, 731 F. Supp. 423 (D. Colo., 1989).

23. *Robbins v. Clarke*, 946 F.2d 1331 (8th Cir. 1991), *Glick v. Henderson*, 855 F.2d 536 (8th Cir. 1988), *Portee v. Tollison*, 753 F. Supp. 184 (D.S.C. 1990).

24. *Henderson v. Sheahan*, 196 F.3d 839 (7th Cir., 1999).

25. *Johnson v. Pearson*, 316 F.Supp.2d 307 (E.D.Vir., 2004) .

26. *Thomas v. Booker*, 762 F.2d 654 (8th Cir., 1985).

Chapter 9:
Suicide

In both prisons and jails, some inmates will attempt suicide. Some will succeed, despite the best efforts of administrators and staff. Lawsuits seem to follow those suicides (and many suicide attempts) almost as night follows day. The suicide problem is particularly significant in jails, where nearly 50 percent of all inmate deaths are suicides, as opposed to about 10 percent in prisons. About three times more suicides occur in jails than in prisons.[1]

Suits claiming both civil rights violations and negligence (or other theories of recovery) under state law, will be brought either by the estate of the deceased and/or by the surviving family. Whatever legal theory may underlie these suits, their basic claims will be the same: some failure on the part of institution staff resulted in the death of the victim and that despite the victim's intention to take his or her own life, the institution in some way should have intervened to prevent the suicide.

The suits will ask for damage awards and these awards can be high. In 1985, the city of Detroit tentatively settled a jail suicide case for $275,000. That same year, a New York City jury awarded $1,000,000 following a suicide attempt that failed. An eighteen-year-old with mental problems who was hallucinating in a jail climbed to the top of a fifteen-foot-high set of bars and dove off, fracturing his skull, partially paralyzing himself, and losing his sense of smell.[2]

While the jury reacted to the facts in the New York case, an appeals court instead reacted to the law and reversed the damage award.[3] The court recognized that the defendants owed a duty of reasonable care to the plaintiff, and that what the defendants must do in a particular case depends on the risk that is reasonably perceived. (In short, the greater the risk that the institution staff perceived or reasonably should have perceived, the more the staff will be expected to have done in response to the risk.) Noting well-developed policies on restraint of inmates (which did not require restraint of a person behaving as the plaintiff), the court ruled the defendants had taken adequate precautions to protect the plaintiff. The staff had taken the victim's belt and shoelaces and placed an officer outside the holding pen.

In July 1986, a jury awarded 2.4 million dollars against the District of Columbia for what could be called a "failure to properly respond" suicide suit.[4] This case shows what a narrow margin of error jail staff may have in avoiding liability. The deceased person had been arrested for drunk driving and placed in a holding cell. He was found hanging shortly thereafter. (The victim lived for more than a year without regaining consciousness.) The jury was convinced that resuscitation efforts did not begin for five minutes after the victim was found. Expert testimony showed irreversible brain damage occurs about eight minutes after oxygen is cut off from the brain. The jury believed that had efforts to revive the victim been begun sooner, he would have been saved. The point of this case is that efforts to revive a suicide victim must be begun virtually instantly, even if the victim appears dead.

In 2006, a Texas county settled a jail suicide case for $300,000. Allegations were that the wife of the deceased inmate had warned jail staff that her husband was suicidal, that the jail was understaffed, that cell checks required by state jail standards were often skipped, and that the inmate was allowed to cover his cell window with paper before committing suicide.[5]

Anyone working in corrections, especially jails, should remember the following basic principles: There will be suicides, and there will be lawsuits about them. The message is clear: forewarned is forearmed. Proper anticipation and preparation for suicide attempts and for subsequent lawsuits not only will reduce the likelihood of successful suicide attempts but also will reduce the likelihood of successful lawsuits.

Theories of Liability: Why Inmates Must Be Protected from Themselves

A suicide does not create liability. Correctional facilities and staff are not no-fault insurers of inmates who attempt suicide. However, correctional staff do have a duty to protect inmates from themselves and, therefore, cannot brush off potential suicide liability simply by saying that "we can't be responsible for what someone does to himself." The key liability question is how the duty to protect is defined and what steps the institution must take to meet the duty the law creates.

Under basic tort law, the custodian has the duty to take "reasonable" steps to protect those in custody. This duty includes using due care to protect inmates from one another as well as to protect inmates from themselves. The duty owed a specific inmate in a specific situation will depend on the facts of the situation— what is reasonable for one inmate not thought to be a serious suicide threat may not be reasonable for the next inmate, whose condition is more serious.[6]

A duty to protect also exists under the Constitution, although courts are not of a single mind: to some, this duty is part of the duty to provide adequate medical care. To others, it is a part of the general duty to protect.[7] While there may be interesting conceptual differences between these two theories, the differences are of greater concern to theoreticians than to practitioners. Under either a medical care or failure-to-protect approach, the question will be whether the defendants were deliberately indifferent to the needs of the inmates.

The deliberate indifference test requires proof of more than simple negligence (the test under most tort theories). If anything, the gap between negligence and deliberate indifference is growing, not shrinking. In 1985, a federal appeals court said that to state a claim under a deliberate indifference theory, there must be a failure to take action when there is a strong likelihood, not a mere possibility, that injury will occur.[8] Since then, numerous other courts have adopted the same "strong likelihood" test.[9]

Case Study: "Deliberate Indifference" Not Easy Burden for Plaintiff

The arrestee—and later suicide victim—came into the jail with prominent scars on his wrists, inside his elbows, and on the back of his neck. These scars were shown to an officer. Failure to recognize these as signs of previous suicide attempts and to take some sort of precautions was, at worst, mere negligence. Even when the arrestee's probation officer, who knew of the suicidal tendencies and prior attempts, visited the offender in the jail but did not inform jail staff about the potential suicide problems, only negligence was shown. With only negligence being proven, the plaintiff failed to show any of the decedent's constitutional rights had been violated. *Freedman v. City of Allentown*, 853 F.2d 1111 (3rd Cir., 1988).

Given the lower legal burden, a plaintiff faces when suing under a tort (negligence) theory, it is likely that an increasing amount of suicide litigation will be brought under a tort theory. However, civil rights claims often will be included, if for no other reasons than to increase the possible ways of recovering and to create a possibility for the plaintiff to recover attorney's fees under 42 USC Section 1983.

Categories of Factual Allegations

The allegations in a suicide case usually focus on one or more of the following areas:

1. Failure to Identify

A failure to identify the victim as a potential suicide and to take proper steps to prevent the suicide is perhaps the most common claim. This claim may arise from such things as a failure of police to tell jail staff of an arrestee's strange behavior at the time of booking or the failure of one institution to tell another institution about an inmate's mental problems at the time the inmate is transferred. Failure on the part of staff to recognize and respond to inappropriate behavior on the part of the inmate also may be raised under this category.

As an example of a "failure-to-identify" type of case, a federal appeals court found the following facts, if proven at trial, could show deliberate indifference on the part of defendants.[10] The suicide victim-to-be was arrested on suspicion of burglary and theft. On the way to the station, he tried to kick out the windows of the police car and hit his head on the divider between the front and rear seats. His father told police the arrestee had had a nervous breakdown. Police failed to tell jail staff any of this information.

Jail staff failed to notice that the victim had been in the jail before and had attempted suicide (information available in jail clinical records). (Of course, jail staff should have searched their own records for this sort of information.) Two medical alert bracelets were noted, one indicating "mental." Despite all this information, no special precautions were taken. Three hours after being booked, the arrestee hanged himself in a solitary cell.[11]

Under these facts, deliberate indifference could have been shown, even though the court noted the plaintiff must show a strong likelihood of injury (not a mere possibility) and that the defendants failed to act in light of this strong possibility. It may be that one cannot show deliberate indifference in failing to identify a potential suicide candidate unless there has been either a previous threat of suicide or an actual previous attempt at suicide.[12]

2. Failure to Monitor

Failure to monitor claims arise after the inmate has been identified as a suicide risk. The claim may be that staff failed to make frequent enough checks or visual or audio monitoring systems are inoperable or ignored by staff expected to be monitoring such systems. How frequently an inmate on "suicide watch" should be checked may vary depending on the inmate. In extreme situations, inmates may have to be kept under constant observation by staff. Single-celling some inmates may provide the basis of a claim, despite all that has been said in favor of single celling in recent years.[13] Putting a potentially suicidal inmate in a cell with another person may help discourage the inmate from attempting suicide and increase the likelihood of a warning to facility staff should a suicide be attempted.

Video surveillance can provide almost illusory protection for the suicidal inmate. For example, an inmate was on a "medical watch," which meant he was supposed to be on constant video surveillance. However, the officer who was responsible for maintaining that surveillance had twenty-seven other cells to monitor on small video screens. Guess who found the inmate who had committed suicide? It was an officer making rounds in the unit, not the officer doing the "monitoring.[14] In another case, the cell being monitored by video had a blind spot that the camera could not see.[15] The obvious risk of video surveillance is that the person assigned to monitor the video is expected to be doing many other tasks as well as monitoring a score or more of video cameras, only one of which shows the potentially suicidal victim. The monitoring that actually takes place is likely to be haphazard and not documented. Video surveillance can be a supplement to frequent, direct "eyeball" contact with the inmate but it should not replace such contact. If video surveillance is used, why not demand that the officer assigned to perform the task consciously check the suicide camera at frequent, designated intervals (such as every five minutes), and log those checks with a brief notation of what was seen?

3. Failure to Respond

A failure to respond properly to the suicide attempt once it is detected may be the basis of a claim. Are staff trained in what to do in the case of a suicide attempt, and do they act in accordance with their training? Is immediate emergency care provided (usually CPR)? Is additional medical care called immediately, and does it arrive in a timely fashion? (Jail staff cannot be held liable for a fire department emergency medical team being delayed in arriving, once called, but liability could be based on the jail's knowledge that emergency medical care is always some time and distance away and then failing to take steps to see that such care can be obtained more quickly.)

Allowing a hanging victim to remain hanging for a substantial period was found to be deliberate indifference to the inmate's serious medical needs, even though the officer thought the inmate was dead. In another case, a seventeen-year-old detainee hanged himself. The police chief, treating the scene as a crime scene, refused to allow officers to cut him down when they found him until the sheriff, prosecutor, and photo unit arrived. The appeals court in that case said it was an error not to allow the jury to hear an expert's opinion on whether the delay in administering CPR was a substantial factor contributing to the death of the youth.[16] The "message" from these cases is that officers need to treat any suicide as a medical emergency and respond as quickly as they can on that basis, consistent with fundamental security concerns in the institution.

Even facility design can become an issue in a suicide case. Early in 2000, the Seventh Circuit considered such a case. There were no allegations that jail staff had failed to watch the arrestee properly. The only claim was that the City of Chicago, which ran the jail, was deliberately indifferent to the safety needs of detainees because its cells were built with horizontal bars. The arrestee had hanged himself from one of these bars. Noting that the state jail standards permitted such construction, and that the plaintiff did not present any evidence showing such construction was contrary to contemporary professional standards, the court ruled in favor of the city.[17]

The New York case mentioned earlier where the inmate dove off the bars included a claim of negligence based on the high-ceilinged design, which allowed the inmate to dive from the height he did. In another case, an inmate hanged himself from overhead bars in the cell. The court there ruled there was no negligence as a matter of law (thus preventing the question of the cell design from even getting to the jury) because the inmate could have hanged himself from bars on the side of the cell, as well. Had there been allegations in the case of bizarre behavior (there were none), putting an inmate in a cell with overhead bars could more easily have made cell design a relevant issue.

Finally, suicide cases may be the sort in which everything but the kitchen sink gets thrown into the complaint. In a Montana case, an arrestee hanged himself within thirty minutes of being booked on three traffic offenses. A suit by the parents alleged violations of the First, Fourth, Fifth, Sixth, Eighth, Ninth, Tenth, and Fourteenth Amendments, as well as state claims of negligence, gross negligence, intentional inflections of emotional distress, and assault and battery.[18] The court of appeals upheld the district court's decision to dismiss the more esoteric claims.

Any of the main three areas (failure to detect, failure to monitor, failure to respond) can be based either on failure of individuals to do what they should or on failure of the system to properly prepare staff for the inevitable suicide attempts. Examples of system failure might include intake screening procedures that did not require booking staff to ask questions that might show an arrestee was suicidal or failure to train staff in recognizing behavioral indicators of potential suicides. Examples of individual failure would include situations where an individual staff member failed to complete a screening questionnaire or failed to observe the inmate frequently enough.

Case Study: Who Makes the Decision to Discharge Someone from Suicide Watch?

Many staff may be able to place an inmate on suicide watch, but removing someone from a suicide watch may require the participation of medical or mental health professionals.

The inmate had tried to kill himself by swallowing cleaner fluid. He had a recent history of mental problems. After several days on suicide watch, the senior staff of the jail, including the jail commander, reviewed the case and agreed he could be released. He almost immediately killed himself. The district court judge said that the failure to include qualified mental health expertise as part of the removal decision was close enough to deliberate indifference to allow the question to go to a jury. *Estate of Cills v. Kaftan*, 105 F.Supp.2d 391 (D.N.J., 2000).

In another case, a court of appeals said an officer assigned to make the suicide watch discharge decision was not deliberately indifferent where she checked facility logs about the inmate's eating, sleeping, and social habits and interviewed and evaluated the inmate in light of her experience but did not consult a mental health expert. Having exonerated the individual officer, the court went on to say that the Policy she followed that allowed an officer to make the removal decision could reflect deliberate indifference. *Yellow Horse v. Pennington County*, 225 F.3d 923 (8th Cir., 2000).

The message from these and other cases is that input from qualified medical mental health professionals may be essential to the decision to take someone off suicide watch.

Preparation: The Key to Liability Prevention

Given that suicide attempts are predictable in a general sense in virtually any correctional facility (especially jails), the failure to have proper policies and procedures relating to identification, monitoring, and responding can be argued to be deliberate indifference and almost certainly would show negligence on the part of administrators.

Particularly important in the jail setting is the procedure for initial screening of persons at the time of booking, since many suicides occur shortly after initial booking.[19] This screening readily can be done by booking officers and does not have to rely on mental health professionals, although obviously the results of such screening could require the prompt involvement of mental health experts. The initial screening should rely on a written screening instrument, of which many are available.[20]

Staff should be trained to recognize potential suicide symptoms, and procedures should exist for the referral of these persons to mental health specialists. Communication between custody staff and mental health staff is of great importance, and must work in both directions. Custody staff need to be able to get information quickly to mental health personnel, and need to be able to get information back from the mental health staff regarding the status of inmates in the cellblock, whether special precautions need to be taken, and so forth.

Monitoring procedures and facilities should be available. If mechanical monitoring (audio, video) is used, it should be kept functional. If an inmate is being monitored at some regular interval, logs should be kept showing the number and times of staff contact. This includes logs of video and audio monitoring. It is dangerous to assume that a person assigned to monitor one of many video screens as well as performing a number of other tasks will regularly check the suicide watch screen. Requiring that the person stop everything else he or she is doing, check the suicide watch screen and log that observation will provide a record that the checks were made. Mechanical monitoring (audio, video) is not a substitute for in-person monitoring.

Staff also should be trained in suicide response and in lifesaving skills, especially CPR. Records should show the training staff have received. Records, in the forms of logs, booking forms, incident reports, and the like also will be of great importance in documenting what staff knew of an inmate, what precautions had been taken (if any), and what the response was to the suicide attempt.

How effective are suicide prevention programs? Some argue that "if an inmate wants to commit suicide, there is nothing we can do to stop him." Jail suicides became a focus of attention in the late 1970s and early 1980s, leading to the development of suicide-prevention programs, suicide screening at booking, improved staff training, and other steps to reduce suicides. In 1983, jail inmates committed suicide at the rate of 129 suicidies/100,000 inmates. In 2002, the rate had fallen to 47/100,000, a decline of 64 percent.[21] This huge drop in jail suicides provides strong testimony that institutional suicides can be reduced.

Case Study: If Something Can Go Wrong, It Will, but Juries Can Be Fickle

A man was arrested and charged with attempted forcible rape. After a few weeks in a Louisiana jail, he told the jail nurse and jail warden that he wanted to die and that someone was trying to kill him. Later that day, he claimed he swallowed a large number of pills, although no one ever determined what he swallowed.

The jail doctor ordered the detainee taken to the hospital, where his stomach was pumped. The doctor classified him as suicidal and recommended he be taken to New Orleans for a psychiatric evaluation, which was done. The psychiatrist prepared a report, put it in an envelope, and gave it to a deputy, who brought the envelope and the inmate back to the jail. The deputy did not know what was in the envelope. He did not give it to anyone at the jail, but simply put it on the booking desk at a time when the warden was in the vicinity.

When the inmate returned to the jail, he punched an officer and tried to escape. The warden promptly put him in solitary confinement, where he committed suicide a short while later. After his death, the envelope was found and opened. The psychiatrist had diagnosed him as suicidal and recommended that suicide precautions be taken. Obviously, none were. Suit was brought by his widow and children.

Using a "deliberate indifference" test, the jury found the man's right to medical care had been violated and that the warden was responsible for the violation. But having found a constitutional violation, the jury awarded only $6,279 damages for funeral costs. *Lewis v. Parish of Terrebone*, 894 F.2d 142 (5th Cir., 1990).

Conclusion

Suicide litigation is one of those areas of litigation where keeping a case away from a jury may be very important. A case in point is the New York case where the jury awarded $1,000,000 to the detainee who dived off the cell bars. The appeals court reversed, holding the defendants were not liable as a matter of law. But the jury, moved by the fact of someone's great injury, wanted to award substantial damages.

Often the suicide victim will be someone arrested for relatively minor offenses, often as a juvenile. In short, the victim may be someone for whom the jury may have a good deal of sympathy. If the victim fits this description, the jury may not be particularly impressed by the jail defendants explaining their policies and procedures and theories of jail management. Yet, if such policies and procedures are in place, records can show staff were trained in them, and that the policies and procedures were followed carefully, a court may be able to rule in the defendants' favor without the case getting to the jury. But any failure in following the best policy may give the plaintiff a "but for" argument and get the case to the jury. For example, "but for" the defendants' failure to start CPR as required by policy, the victim suffered prolonged lack of oxygen to the brain and eventually died.

The duties jail and prison administrators have toward protecting persons in their custody from themselves are relatively clear. Winning or losing a suicide suit then will depend on the facts of the case: Did the staff know what they were supposed to do, and did they do it?

Review Questions

1. Name two types of legal actions that could be brought following a suicide.

2. What are the three factual claims most likely to appear in a suicide case?

3. Give two examples of where an individual officer's failures could provide the basis for a suicide lawsuit.

Endnotes

1. Cohen, Fred. *Sourcebook on the Mentally Disordered Offender*, National Institute of Corrections, 1985. p. 67. For additional data about jail suicides, *see* Hayes and Rowan, *National Study of Jail Suicides: Seven Years Later*, National Center on Institutions and Alternatives, February 1988.

2. *Jail and Prisoner Law Bulletin*, March 1985 and January 1986.

3. *Gordon v. City of New York*, 502 NYS 2d 215 (Supreme Court App. Div., 1986).

4. 117 *Jail and Prison Law Bulletin*, September 1986. p. 11.

5. *Prison Law News*, October 2006. p. 33.

6. *Civil Liability of Prison or Jail Authorities for Self-Inflicted Injury or Death of Prisoners*, 79 ALR 3rd 1210 (1977).

7. *Partridge v. Two Unknown Police Officers*, 751 F.2d 1448 (5th Cir., 1985). For sentenced inmates, the claim under either theory would be made under the Eighth Amendment (cruel and unusual punishment). For pretrial detainees, the claim would arise under the Fourteenth Amendment (due process). The functional test under either Eighth or Fourteenth Amendments would be basically the same.

8. *Partridge*, 751 F.2d at 1453.

9. *Torraco v. Maloney*, 923 F.2d 231 (1st Cir., 1991), *Gregoire v. Class*, 236 F.3d 413 (8th Cir., 2000).

10. *Partridge*, see endnote 7.

11. Use of single cells for potential suicide victims, unless extraordinary staffing measures are taken, has been criticized. Multiple celling has been shown to reduce suicides, although obviously it can create other problems. Rowan, *Monograph of Suicide Prevention*, Juvenile and Criminal Justice International, Inc. Rowan was the former director of the American Medical Association's Jail Project.

12. *Edwards v. Gilbert*, 867 F.2d 1271 (11th Cir., 1989).

13. *See* endnote 6.

14. *Heflin v. Stewart County*, 958 F.2d 709 (6th Cir., 1992), *Hake v. Manchester Township*, 486 A.2d 836 (N.J., 1985).

15. *Frake v. City of Chicago*, 2000 WL 433568, (7th Cir., 2000).

16. *Brown v. Harris*, 240 F.3d 383 (4th Cir., 2000).

17. *Popham v. City of Talladega*, 908 F.2d 1561 (11th Cir., 1990).

18. *Strandberg v. City of Helena*, 791 F.2d 744 (9th Cir., 1986).

19. Rowan and Hayes, *Training Curriculum On Suicide Detection and Prevention In Jails and Lockups*, National Center on Institutions and Alternatives, February 1988.

20. *See* Rowan and Hayes, endnote 16. The National Commission on Correctional Health Care (NCCHC), American Correctional Association, the National Sheriff's Association, and the American Jail Association have information on screening programs and jail suicide prevention.

21. U.S. Department of Justice, Press Release, Aug. 21, 2005. This huge drop in jail suicides provides strong testimony to the idea that institutional suicides can be reduced.

Chapter 10:
Use of Force

Correctional officers are authorized to use force against inmates in appropriate circumstances. In some circumstances, even deadly force may be used. However, the legal power to use force is limited by both statute and case law. The improper use of force can expose the officer—and perhaps the agency—to liability. Force may not be used to punish inmates; agency rules uniformly prohibit the use of force as punishment. The officer or officers who surreptitiously beat inmates "to teach them a lesson" invite agency discipline against themselves (probably termination), as well as lawsuits by the inmate. Supervisors who turn a blind eye to this sort of improper force also may find themselves at the wrong end of a lawsuit for failing to properly supervise officers.

Use-of-force claims can be brought as torts or as civil rights actions. As a tort, the claim would be brought in state court and probably would be characterized as "assault and battery." The claim would be that the force was not authorized under state law or, that while some force was proper, the amount used was excessive.

Brought as a civil rights action, a use-of-force claim would assert that a constitutional right had been violated. For convicted persons, the claim would be brought under the Eighth Amendment—the force used constituted cruel and unusual punishment. For pretrial detainees (who are not protected by the Eighth Amendment), the claim would arise under the Fourteenth Amendment (due process).

Under either an Eighth or Fourteenth Amendment analysis, the basic questions are the same. In either situation, the court must consider two questions, one objective, one subjective. The objective question considers the seriousness of the injury the inmate suffered. Generally speaking, if the inmate suffers no injury or only a minor injury (a "*de minimis*" injury, in legal parlance), the inmate's claim fails.

If the inmate's claim meets the objective test, then a court will consider the subjective question. Here, the question is "whether force was applied in a good-faith effort to maintain or restore discipline, or maliciously and sadistically to cause harm."[2] Courts are split on whether their focus should be on the first or second half of this test. One circuit takes the position that if force is not used in a good-faith effort to maintain or restore discipline, it is virtually then by definition malicious and sadistic.[3] Another court has said that "there is no room for qualified immunity" in Eighth and Fourteenth Amendment excessive force cases because they require a subjective element that is "so extreme" that no reasonable person could believe that his or her actions were lawful.[4] Other circuits focus more heavily on the nature of the force, trying to determine if it amounts to malicious and sadistic conduct.[5] More discussion of the constitutional test for evaluating use-of-force claims appears below.

Justifying Force

When is force justified? In general, force may be appropriate when, in the eyes of a reasonable correctional officer, there are no other available alternatives, and the force is used for the following reasons:

- In self-defense

- To protect others or to protect property

- To enforce prison rules and discipline

- To prevent a crime, including escapes

Deadly force requires special comment. Because of the potential consequences—loss of life—any time deadly force is used, its proper use is more limited than nondeadly force. Because of the seriousness of the potential consequences, staff need to be very familiar with the limitation(s) in agency policy about the use of deadly force.

Deadly force may be used in self-defense and in the protection of others from death or serious bodily harm and, in at least some cases, in the prevention of escape. Deadly force generally may not be used for the protection of property.

While it is easy to state the principles of when force may be used, it is much more difficult to provide clear guidance as to how those principles would be applied in particular cases. The basic rules listed above are not absolute. For instance, force is not always proper as a tool to enforce institutional rules, when alternatives less than force would have gotten the job done adequately. In addition, if some force is proper, that does not mean that any amount of force is proper. While physically escorting an inmate away from a disturbance (technically, a use of force) is proper, it is not proper to strike the inmate repeatedly with a baton unless there is a sound reason for using the baton.

Most excess force litigation looks at the following basic questions:

1. Was there a need for force in the first place?

2. If some force was appropriate, was the *amount used* appropriate?

3. If force was not appropriate and/or the amount used was excessive, was the amount used so excessive as to violate the Constitution or state law?

Case Study: Force and Enforcing Rules

The principle that force can be used to enforce facility rules has its limits, as an officer in an Arkansas jail learned too late. An inmate refused to sweep his cell, displaying something of an attitude in his refusal. After warning the inmate, an officer fetched the stun gun and used it on the inmate who then cleaned his cell. The court was, one could say, shocked by this use of electricity against the inmate since there was no showing that the inmate presented an immediate danger to anyone or anything and the officers did not attempt to restrain or move the inmate after using the stun gun. The lower court's judgment in favor of the officer was reversed and the case remanded for damages to be set. The court felt the evidence showed the stun gun was used simply as a means of inflicting a painful punishment on the inmate. *Hickey v. Reeder*, 12 F.3d 754 (8th Cir., 1993).

In 1992, the Supreme Court reviewed a use-of-force case, *Hudson v. McMillian*, discussed earlier, that arose out of a beating that occurred in a Louisiana prison. The trial court found that one officer had held an inmate being moved in the institution while another officer kicked and punched the inmate, who had been offering no resistance and was in handcuffs and shackles. A supervisor observed the incident, but did nothing to intervene, and, in fact, the court found the supervisor had expressly condoned the force being used. The court also found there was absolutely no need for force being used and that the officers were motivated by malice. The inmate sustained some injuries, but they were not serious. He was awarded $800 in damages.

133

The court of appeals reversed the district court decision. It felt that unless the inmate could show he had sustained a "significant injury," he could not prove that he had been subjected to cruel and unusual punishment, regardless of how unnecessary the force was.

The Supreme Court reversed, saying that it was error to insist that a beating victim prove "significant injury" in order to state a claim for relief.[6] The Court said that in excess-force cases, the proper question was whether the inmate had suffered the "wanton and unnecessary infliction of pain."

The Court further defined the phrase "wanton and unnecessary infliction of pain," saying that in situations involving the use of force, which often may be emergencies (although the facts of the *Hudson* case did not involve an emergency), the question is "whether force was applied in a good faith effort to maintain or restore discipline or maliciously and sadistically for the very purpose of causing harm."[7] This test maximizes the discretion available to institution officials and minimizes the extent to which courts can review use-of-force situations. The Court further explained its "malicious and sadistic" test by indicating five factors, which a court should evaluate in reviewing a force incident:

1. Was there a need to use any force?

2. What was the amount of force used?

3. What injuries were inflicted, if any? (While significant injury is not required, the extent of any injuries is relevant and should be considered. The inmate who suffers little if any injury will have a difficult time winning an excess force case. Questions about the nature and extent of injuries are important in deciding if the inmate's claim meets the objective component in the use-of-force analysis).

4. What was the threat perceived by responsible correctional officials?

5. What efforts were made to temper the use of force?

The *Hudson* decision took its "malicious and sadistic" test from an earlier Supreme Court decision, which created and applied the test in the setting of a prison riot.[8] Application of this test outside the riot-emergency context, especially in a case which involved officers beating an inmate, was surprising because the effect of the *Hudson* decision is to reduce judicial oversight of use-of-force incidents. A use-of-force incident could be criticized under all five of the factors identified in the *Hudson* case yet still not sink to the level of being "malicious and sadistic." However, excessive use of force still may violate the rights of inmates.

Kneeing an inmate twice in the groin as a first response to the inmate's aggressiveness during booking, instead of using other more humane means of physical restraint, violated the rights of the inmate and led to a damage award of more than $56,000, including $25,000 in punitive damages.[9] In another case, a court of appeals said that an officer's use of a stun gun against an inmate locked in his cell as a response to the inmate's refusal to clean his cell violated the rights of the inmate.[10]

As a practical matter, a court analyzing an excess-force claim under the test from the *Hudson* case usually makes up its mind after considering the first three of the five important factors listed in *Hudson*. Thus, if there is only a *de minimus* injury, the claim fails on the "injury" question. Or, if there is a clear relationship between the need for some force and the amount actually used, the claim will typically fail. On the "need" and "amount" questions, which are closely related, officers who follow a well-established force continuum are in a very good position to defend their of force.

Many correctional agencies have adopted a "force continuum" to provide guidance to staff in force situations. The continuum indicates what the officer's range of appropriate response alternatives are when an inmate's behavior falls into one of several broad categories. Thus, if the inmate is passively resistive, the officer's range of alternatives is more limited than if the inmate is engaged in life-threatening behavior. By acting consistently with the agency's force continuum, the officer usually will be able to say "my actions were taken in accordance with agency policy, which, in turn, reflects a carefully thought out way of balancing the amount of force used against the need for the use of force."

The "efforts to temper" factor under the *Hudson* case can consider two different situations. The first is what steps an officer(s) took to avoid the use of force in the first instance. For example in a cell-extraction situation, what did the officers do to try to convince the inmate to come out of his cell voluntarily? Did they try to wait the inmate out? Did one or more staff try to talk to the inmate? Was the inmate warned clearly of the consequences of continuing to refuse to comply with orders, and so forth? Courts rarely get into this sort of analysis although obviously it is important to the officers and the agency since every time staff defuse a potential force incident by talking, they avoid the risk of injury to themselves and the inmate as well as the time, expense, risk of litigation, and possible liability that can come from any force incident.

The second situation is what steps officers took as the force incident was winding down. Consider this example. An inmate, Kevin Danley, got into an argument with officers over a lack of toilet paper. One of three officers involved in moving him from one cell to another told him to be quiet or she would "spray him." The inmate asked what she meant and so she showed him, spraying him with OC for three-to-five seconds. The officers then pushed Danley back into a small cell and left him with OC on him, on his clothes, and in the air in the small, poorly ventilated cell. The inmate began having trouble breathing and "screamed and cried to the three jailers that he could not breathe." They ignored his plea for assistance, made a "mock-choking" gesture and told him that unless he shut up, they would not let him out.

Danley quieted down in about ten minutes, but the jail staff left him in the cell for another ten minutes. They, then, took him out and gave him a two-minute shower, which he said was not long enough to let him get rid of the OC and which was less than agency policy required. The OC also was still on his clothes. Danley said he continued to have trouble breathing after being returned to a large group cell, and that his eyes burned and swelled. Danley was later moved to a better ventilated cell but was not given any other decontamination before his release from the jail, about twelve hours later.

The complaint in Danley's subsequent Section 1983 suit alleged that the jail administrator and the sheriff had a de facto policy of allowing jail staff to punish inmates through the use/misuse of OC.

The defendants moved to dismiss the case on qualified immunity grounds, asserting that if they violated any of Danley's rights, the rights were not clearly established and, therefore, they were immune from damages. The district court denied the motion and the court of appeals agreed that the complaint stated a claim against all of the defendants.[11] The court of appeals saw no problem with the use of the OC following Danley's twice refusing to obey the officer's orders. There was a need for force, the amount was reasonable, the injuries not that serious, and Danley's behavior created a disturbance to which the OC was a reasonable response. However, the officers failed to attempt to temper the use of OC by not allowing Danley to decontaminate himself and locking him in the small cell, heavy with OC residue.

"When jailers continue to use substantial force against a prisoner who has clearly stopped resisting—whether because he has decided to become compliant, he has been subdued, or he is otherwise incapacitated—that use of force is excessive."[12] The court said the pepper spray did what it was intended to do—it subdued or disabled the unruly inmate. However, once the inmate was back in the small cell, the spray's work was done. Yet, the actions of the officers in effect resulted in the continued use of OC when there was no need to do so. The *failure to decontaminate* the inmate became a type of excessive force. Other aspects of the officers' alleged behavior, such as mocking Danley and not allowing him the time to decontaminate called for by agency policy, helped lead the court to the conclusion that the officers were acting maliciously and sadistically and thus violating Danley's rights to be free from excessive force.

Case Study: Unchecked Use of Force Creates Liability for Agency, Not Just Officers

No one is happy until they get their morning coffee or so it seems. An inmate mouthed off to an officer about not getting his coffee. When the officer did not respond, the inmate reached through the bars and pushed the officer in the back. The officer then responded by getting a fire hose and hosing the inmate, who remained the entire time locked in his single cell. Other officers squirted tear gas on the inmate and beat him with nightsticks. Sixty-nine stitches were required to repair the damage.

This force violated the rights of the inmate. Evidence also showed that the warden condoned the use of fire hoses against inmates in single cells who did not present any direct threat to staff. The warden once had approved hosing a handcuffed inmate locked in a cell. Recommendations from a special commission to discontinue using fire hoses were rejected. While it was not completely clear if the head of the agency knew of the use of fire hoses, it was clear he should have. Under these circumstances, both the warden and the agency director were found liable, along with the officers actually involved in the incident. The inmate was awarded more than $32,000 in damages. *Slakan v. Porter*, 737 F.2d 368 (4th Cir., 1984).[13]

Weapons, Special Holds, and "Inherently Dangerous Instrumentalities"

Batons, gas, Tasers*, stun belts, hoses, choke or sleeper holds, or other special forms of manual or physical restraint may not be classified as deadly force, but they still may carry the potential for serious injury or even death. If used properly, they can reduce the risk of injury to both the officer and the inmate. They are, however, capable of being abused and becoming a means of improperly punishing the inmate.

*The word Taser is a registered trademark of Taser® International of Scottsdale, Arizona.

In the case study on unchecked force, one of the reasons the court imposed liability against the agency director was due to the lack of any policy describing the use of what the court called "inherently dangerous instrumentalities," such as the fire hoses. Firearms and other instruments that have the potential of inflicting very serious harm also would be included in the category of "inherently dangerous instrumentalities." The law may give staff using such techniques or instruments an especially high duty to use them properly. So, a lawsuit might focus on two some-what different questions: (1) was there a sufficient justification to use, for instance, a firearm? and (2) was the firearm used in a careful way? The person who might bring the latter claim is the innocent bystander who was shot by mistake.

Sometimes an injury or death may result from a practice that no one realized was dangerous. What if an inmate dies after being hit with a Taser? Neck holds, now usually seen as a form of deadly force, were not previously classified as such. Only after several inmates died as a result of neck holds did many agencies classify neck holds as deadly force. If no notice were given that the practice was likely to cause such death or injury, liability is not likely. However, after death or injury occurs once, is an agency on notice about the practice? What if death occurs a second time? The more times the "unexpected" occurs (such as death resulting from the use of neck holds), the more an agency will be expected to be aware that special precautions and training may be necessary.

Tasers

Tasers provide a good example of a force tool that may come to be considered an "inherently dangerous instrumentality." As Taser usage has grown, particularly by police, a number of deaths has been associated with the instrument. A substantial controversy swirls around whether the Taser was or was not a contributing factor to those deaths.

In June of 2008, the National Institute of Justice released a *Study of Deaths Following Electro Muscular Disruption: Interim Report.* The study used the generic term "conducted energy devices" (CEDs) for what the field commonly refers to as Tasers.[12] In general, the report found that there was no medical evidence that CEDs posed a high risk of serious injury or death but that the safety margins for CED use in "normal healthy adult may not be applicable in small children, those with diseased hearts, the elderly, those who are pregnant and other at-risk individuals."[13] The report cautioned that there are unknowns that remain regarding use of CEDs and that "caution is urged in using multiple activations of CEDs as a means to" subdue someone.[14]

Police use of a Taser provides a cautionary example of the "multiple-activation" situation. A police officer was attempting to arrest a suspect. The officer "tased" the individual five times in about seventy-five seconds as the suspect refused the officer's order to lie on his stomach and extend his arms. The suspect was on the ground for four of the five tasings. The trial court found that while the first three tasings were appropriate, the last two violated the constitutional rights of the suspect. The court was influenced by the arrival of a second officer, which reduced the threat to the lone officer and opened up alternatives less painful than the Taser. After finding a constitutional violation, the court concluded that the law regarding the use of the Taser was not clearly established and granted the officer qualified immunity from damages.[16]

Another multiple-Taser use case comes from Alabama. A suspect was in a small room in the jail with an arresting officer who was participating in the booking process and two other officers. The suspect refused several orders to put on his clothes and became agitated but did not make any aggressive moves toward any of the officers. The arresting officer abruptly pulled out his Taser and pushed it against the suspect and fired it four times. The jail officer in the room told the officer "that was enough" at one point, but the officer retorted "that ain't enough until I say so."[17] The court concluded the tasing violated the arrestee's constitutional rights. He was unarmed, surrounded by three police officers, and made no threatening movements toward the officers. His verbal obstreperousness was not sufficient to justify use of the Taser as a means of enforcing compliance with orders.

While this case involved a Taser, its results are not extraordinary. What if the officer began striking the inmate with a baton as a means of enforcing his order? In that situation, the inappropriate use of force would be obvious. Seen in that light, this is simply a case involving the inappropriate use of force.

There are a couple of messages about Taser usage. One is that the question of whether Tasers are inherently dangerous remains unresolved. The other, of much more immediate importance to officers using Tasers, is that abuse of the instrument, like abuse of any other force technique, can result in liability.

Restraints

Inmates may be restrained physically for good cause. However, restraints should be used in accordance with a carefully drawn policy and their use closely monitored to assure they are not being used improperly. Where it appears restraints are being used for excessively long periods or applied in ways that may injure an inmate or inflict unnecessary pain, courts have intervened. For example: Following a suicide attempt, an inmate was "hog-tied" in three-point restraints in a squatting position and left that way for a week. The court said that the prolonged use of the three-way restraints following the inmate's suicide attempt, plus the lack of medical review or treatment and denial of even basic amenities such as personal hygiene and toilet usage, violated the inmate's rights. Compensatory damages were imposed against various individual officers, and punitive damages were imposed on the official responsible for operation of the jail and against the county.[18]

Areas of concern regarding use of restraints include (1) the decision to place an inmate in restraints: who makes it, and in accordance with what criteria? (2) the types of restraints used, (3) length of time an inmate remains in restraints, (4) monitoring both to determine if the need remains for restraints and of the inmate's general safety, comfort, hygiene, and medical/mental health condition.

As with many other areas of institutional operation that involve inmate rights, protection against successful claims regarding improper use of restraints will depend on having a sound policy or other written directives, which provide guidance for staff, training for staff around the requirements of the policy, documentation regarding uses of force, and strong supervision to assure that the policy is followed properly.

Case Study: Hog-Tying and the Mentally Disturbed Inmate

A short, heavy, middle-aged man was arrested for bizarre, threatening behavior. Police recognized him as probably mentally disturbed, and he was a regular at the jail. He passively refused to cooperate in the booking process. One officer began to physically move the man back to the booking station when another ordered "take him down." Several officers then took the man to the ground and put him in a "kick-stop restraint," a device which tied his hands and feet together behind his back. The court's opinion does not indicate officers made any attempt to deal with the inmate short of immediately placing him in restraints, nor does the response appear to have taken into consideration the man's history of mental problems, although his behavior was clearly abnormal and jail staff knew his history.

Although the kick-stop restraint was commonly used in the jail, none of the officers or supervisors had been trained in use of the device nor were they aware that the manufacturer cautioned against placing a person in the device face down because of a risk of suffocation. A video showed a supervisor placing his weight on the arrestee's back while other officers bound the man's hands and feet together. Within minutes after the man was hogtied and placed in a cell, he was dead. Medical experts testified this caused the man's death by asphyxiation. Other manufacturer's cautions were ignored.

The man's estate filed suit against the city that operated the jail and a large number of individual officers. After a twenty-seven-day trial, the jury returned a damages verdict of nearly $10,000,000 against all of the defendants jointly. In addition, the jury entered punitive damage awards against eight individual defendants, in amounts ranging from $225,000 to $1,000,000. In total, the damage awards came to nearly 13 million dollars! *Swans v. City of Lansing*, 65 F. Supp. 2d 625 (W.D. Mich., 1998).

Deadly Force and Escapes

Courts have not given clear guidance on the question of the use of deadly force to prevent escapes. Perhaps the largest issue, which is not yet clearly resolved, is whether deadly force can be used to prevent any escape (perhaps assuming no other alternative is immediately available) or whether some assessment must be made about the dangerousness of the inmate attempting to escape. Obviously, asking the officer in most escape situations to make such an assessment is to impose a very difficult task on the officer, who may know nothing about the inmate, except that he is trying to escape. One reason for this uncertainty is that there have been very few cases involving the use of deadly force against escapees. Another reason is that different legal tests are used to review any use-of-force claim depending on the person against whom the force is used: a suspect (Fourth Amendment), an arrestee (Fourth Amendment), a pretrial detainee (Fourteenth Amendment), or a convicted inmate (Eighth Amendment).[18]

Questions of state law may further complicate the legal analysis of use of deadly force. For example, under the laws of one state, it is justifiable homicide for a peace officer to use deadly force (and kill an inmate) to prevent the escape of an inmate from a prison or jail. However, the statute says that deadly force generally may not be used against an escaping jail inmate unless the inmate was "arrested for, charged with, or convicted of a felony."[19] This sort of issue should be addressed in the agency's deadly force policies.

141

Use of deadly force not only raises potential liability issues regarding the person the force is used against, but it also can involve liability issues regarding other persons who may be injured by a shot that misses its intended target or a bullet that ricochets. The legal uncertainty in this area can be confusing for staff who may be expected to use deadly force. In light of this confusion, the best advice for the officer with deadly force responsibilities is to be very familiar with guidelines in facility policies regarding the use of deadly force.

Documentation

The quality of records an agency keeps may be critical in defending a use-of-force case. The details of any use-of-force incident are important to the supervisor of the officer(s) involved in the incident so the supervisor can be sure the force was used appropriately. (Ignoring abusive use of force can expose the supervisor to liability.) Should there be a lawsuit filed, the records can help the officer remember what happened during the incident and even may be entered as evidence at trial. Therefore, detailed use-of-force reports can be essential to protect the officer.

Three different types of records can be important.

1. **Incident reports.** First and foremost, officers involved in a use-of-force incident should prepare detailed reports of their actions. These reports should address not only why force was used, but also should describe the actual amount used. However, to be useful the reports, must be detailed. Simply writing that "only necessary force was used" is of no benefit since such a phrase only states the officer's opinion. What is important is that the officer preparing the report include enough detail so that the reader of the report (be it a supervisor, a judge, or a jury) can draw an opinion from the report itself as to whether force was properly used at all and whether the amount used was appropriate under the circumstances. Reports that do not allow this sort of third-party evaluation should be returned to the officer for rewriting.

2. **Videotapes.** Since the late 1970s, many agencies videotape all use-of-force incidents where time and circumstances allow. A videotape shows precisely the amount of force used and can be very impressive to a judge or jury.

   While the videotape in the kick-stop restraint case discussed earlier in this chapter was used successfully against officers, this is the exception. It is far more common that a video will show that officers acted properly. Many administrators also say that the presence of the video camera helps deter some officers from using excessive force. Even where there are not lawsuits about force usage, videotapes give the administrator an excellent tool for evaluating uses of force against the expectations of agency policy.

3. **Medical records.** It is common to have inmates promptly examined by medical personnel immediately after force is used on the inmate. This examination serves two purposes. It gives the inmate prompt treatment for any injuries, reducing the likelihood of a suit regarding delayed or denied medical care. It also gives the institution an accurate record of any injuries (or the lack of any injuries). This evidence can be useful in rebutting later inmate claims about serious injury.

While strong documentation can be very important in defending a force case, as well as other types of inmate lawsuits, poor documentation can be very harmful. If a jury decides that officers "cooked" reports, or that a report has been falsified, the officers will lose almost all credibility. If a report or document that is required to be prepared is not found in the file, an informal presumption arises that it was not prepared. "If it isn't written down, it didn't happen" is not always true, but often is.

Case Study: Falsified Report Leads To Federal Conviction

The consequences of falsifying a report can be more serious than just internal discipline. Just ask the Alabama police officer who was sentenced to five months in federal prison for falsifying a report about a force incident.[20] What happened to the police officer could just as easily happen to a correctional officer.

There was an altercation between several officers and a drug suspect. A decision was made to arrest the suspect and one officer grabbed him and threw him to the pavement. The suspect injured his head, spent eight days in the hospital, and suffered permanent hearing loss.

The officer's report said the suspect grabbed him and tried to slam him, but the officer was able to get his hands free and "take [the suspect] to the ground."

Some time after the incident, the U.S. Department of Justice started an investigation to determine if there had been a violation of the suspect's civil rights. An FBI agent interviewed the officer, who insisted his report was correct. Two days later, the agent conducted a second interview and confronted the officer with a number of inconsistencies in his report. At that point, the officer admitted the report was incorrect.

The officer was convicted of violating a federal statute that prohibits making a false statement in a report with the intent to impede a federal investigation.[21]

He was sentenced to five months' imprisonment and five months' home confinement. Note that the report was written before a federal investigation had been begun. There was evidence that the officer had been trained that the Justice Department would investigate possible civil rights violations and that this knowledge was a key factor in supporting his conviction.

The fact that the officer continued to defend his false report in the first FBI interview also was an important factor in the case. The case does not indicate whether the officer was convicted of violating the suspect's civil rights, whether his agency had disciplined him for the report, or how the reports from other officers involved in the incident described what happened.

Can Force Be Avoided?

The best way to avoid a use-of-force lawsuit is to avoid using force. While obviously force is the only alternative in some situations, in many instances the officer or officers with interpersonal skills can de-escalate a situation and avoid any use of force, even though legally the use of force might have been justified. Likewise, an officer whose interpersonal skills are weak actually may worsen a situation and create the need for force when it could have been avoided. Any time force is used, both the inmate and the officers involved are at risk. The greater the officer's skill in resolving situations without the use of any force, the more the safety of all concerned is increased.

144

Conclusion

Some legal uncertainties remain regarding the use of force (such as the questions around using deadly force to prevent escapes). However, the fundamental principles governing almost all use-of-force situations for line staff are clear.

1. Policies should govern use of force and should be carefully followed.

2. Force may not be used for punishment.

3. Force only should be used when there are no other reasonable alternatives under the situation.

4. Documentation describing use-of-force incidents is important and should be carefully reviewed by supervisors.

5. A court reviewing use-of-force situations generally will examine those from the perspective of a reasonable correctional officer, acting in light of the facts as they appeared to the officer who actually used the force.

A final point to remember in considering use-of-force issues is that because excessive use of force can seriously injure or even kill an inmate, there is a potential for extremely high damage awards in force cases. Force can also be so excessive as to violate the criminal law and expose the officer to possible criminal prosecution and imprisonment.

Review Questions

1. May deadly force be used to protect property?

2. In a constitutional excess force case, what five questions will a court ask?

3. Give two reasons why detailed use-of-force reports are important.

Endnotes

1. For a more detailed discussion see C. Hemmens and Eugene Atherton. 1999. *Use of Force: Current Practice and Policy.* Alexandria, Virginia: American Correctional Association.

2. *Hudson v. McMillian*, 112 S.Ct. 995 (1992).

3. *Blyden v. Mancusi*, 186 F.3d 252, 262 (2d Cir., 1999).

4. Danley v. Allen, 540 F.3d 1298 (11th Cir., 2009).

5. *Fuentes v. Wagner*, 206 F.3d 335 (3rd Cir., 2000).

6. *Hudson v. McMillan*, 112 S.Ct. 995 (1992).

7. 112 S.Ct. at 998.

8. *Whitley v. Albers*, 106 S.Ct. 1078 (1986).

9. *Culver* by and through *Bell v. Fowler*, 862 F.Supp. 369 (M.D. Ga., 1994).

10. *Hickey v. Reeder*, 12 F.3d 754 (8th Cir., 1993).

11. *Danley v. Allen*, 540 F.3d 1298 (11th Cir., 2009).

12. 540 F.3d at 1309.

13. Note that this case was decided in 1984. Since that time, the Supreme Court has decided that individuals cannot be held liable on the basis of what they "should have known." *See* the discussion of *Farmer v. Brennan*, 511 U.S. 825 (1994) in Chapter 8.

14. Interim Report, p. 2.

15. Id.

16. *Beaver v. City of Federal Way*, 507 F.Supp. 2d 1137 (W.D. Wa., 2007), aff'd 2008, U.S. App. LEXIS 26547 (9th Cir. Wash., Nov. 25, 2008).

17. *Stephens v. City of Butler*, 509 F. Supp 2d 1098, 1104, (S.D. Ala., 2007) aff'd 261 Fed. Appx. 240 (5th Cir., 2008).

18. *Jones v. Thompson*, 818 F. Supp. 1263 (S.D. Ind., 1993).

19. See Boston, John and Daniel Manville. 2010. *Prisoner's Self-Help Litigation Manual, 4th ed.* Oceana Publications. Revised Code of Washington, Section 9A.16.040(c)(iii).

20. *U.S. v. Hunt*, 526 F.3d 739 (11th Circuit, 2008).

21. 18 U.S.C. §1519, which states in part: Whoever knowingly alters, destroys, mutilates, conceals, covers up, falsifies, or makes a false entry in any record document, or tangible object with the intent to impede, obstruct, or influence the investigation or proper administration of any matter within the jurisdiction of any department or agency of the United States . . ., or in relation to or contemplation of any such matter or case, shall [violate the statute].

Chapter 11:
The Fourteenth Amendment:
Due Process and Equal Protection

The Fourteenth Amendment to the U.S. Constitution reads, in part:

> . . . nor shall any state deprive any person of life, liberty, or property, without due process of law; nor deny to any person within its jurisdiction the equal protection of the laws.

In other words, when the state (which includes cities and counties) proposes to take away someone's life, liberty, or property, the state must provide "due process of law" to the subject of the proposed deprivation. Usually, this means the state must go through certain procedures as part of the deprivation decision (the "process" that is "due").

The concept of equal protection means generally that groups of persons that are similar must be treated similarly by the government, unless the government can justify treating the similar groups differently. Thus, equal protection does not outlaw discrimination between groups, but does demand that discrimination be justified. Depending on what the reason for discriminating between two like groups is, it may be very difficult for the state to justify the discrimination. For instance, racial discrimination is very difficult to justify. Yet, treating offenders differently based on their prior criminal records would not be as difficult to justify.

The concepts of due process and equal protection entered the U.S. Constitution as far as the states were concerned after the Civil War, and are intended to assure that the government treats persons fairly. The amendment largely deals with how decisions are made that affect the life, liberty, or property of persons in this country. However, it also sometimes simply prohibits some government actions and demands that similar groups of persons be treated the same, unless the government can justify treating them differently.

The Fourteenth Amendment applies only to the states—it does not regulate the power of the federal government. However, the Fifth Amendment to the Constitution also has a due process clause that does apply to the federal government.

Procedural Due Process in General

Most due-process issues involve what is called procedural due process. This concept focuses on what procedures must accompany the decision to take away life, liberty, or property. When a court is concerned about procedural due process, it is far more concerned with the procedural steps the state goes through in making a decision than with what the final decision is. (It is not what you do, but how you do it.)

The goal of procedural due process is fairness. This is done by requiring the state to go through certain procedures (which usually involve notice to the person of the proposed deprivation and some form of a hearing). Then, the person is protected from arbitrary actions of government, actions that perhaps have no factual justification or that simply may be illegal. By going through certain procedures, the following can be determined better:

- If the facts really are as the government claims them to be (For example, did the inmate really violate a disciplinary rule, or did a parolee really violate a condition of parole?)

- If the government has the legal authority to make the deprivation it proposes (For example, do institution rules allow a loss of good time to be imposed as a penalty for violating a particular rule?)

The amount of process required varies from one type of situation to another. Just as with other constitutional rights, courts try to balance the individual's interest in having more procedural rights and the severity of the potential loss the person is facing against the government's interest in being able to make decisions quickly and efficiently. Under this balancing approach, the procedural protections that protect the person facing civil commitment as being mentally ill and dangerous to others (a severe loss of liberty) are much greater than those afforded a parolee in a parole-revocation hearing (parole is seen as only a form of conditional liberty). The protections afforded an inmate in a prison or jail disciplinary hearing are even less than in a parole-revocation hearing.

In general, the greater the potential loss the individual faces, the greater the need for more procedural protections to assure that sufficient factual and legal reasons exist to justify the loss. Outside an institutional setting, a free person normally would expect the following sorts of procedural protections to be available if the government attempted to take away the person's liberty or property:

- A hearing, at which the government would have to prove its case for deprivation

- Advance notice of the hearing, including some detail of the charges, so the person could have time to prepare a defense to the charges

- A neutral judge or other decision maker

- The right to call witnesses on his or her own behalf

- The right to cross-examine witnesses testifying against the person

- The right to the assistance of a lawyer

- A decision that indicates what facts the decision maker is relying on and that gives reasons to justify it (this decision would either be in writing or maintained in some form of oral record that could be reproduced.)

- An appeal of the decision to higher authority, usually the courts

When Is "Process" Due?

Every procedural due process issue begins with the same question: Does the Fourteenth Amendment apply to a particular type of decision that affects an inmate? Does the decision involve potentially taking a liberty or property interest away from the inmate? Inmates have very few "property interests" in prison, so the most common question is whether a decision deprives an inmate of a "liberty interest." As is discussed in detail in the next section, inmate discipline is the most common area where due process protections must be followed. However, what about other types of decisions which, in at least some respects, could be seen as taking away something of value to the inmate? These might include placing the inmate in administrative segregation (where conditions and privileges are typically very similar to disciplinary segregation), or removing an inmate from a program, or transferring the inmate from one institution to another.

The question of "when is process due" also has been a frustrating one for officials, since the Supreme Court has not been consistent in the way it answers the question. Some actions of correctional officials, such as involuntarily medicating a mentally ill inmate, are inherently protected by the due process clause of the Fourteenth Amendment.[1] Most decisions that affect an inmate do not rise to this level of significance, but they still may be protected by due process, if the state has created a liberty interest.

In 1983, the Supreme Court said that to determine if the state had created a liberty interest around a particular type of decision (such as the decision to place an inmate in administrative segregation), courts must examine the language of the institution rules governing that decision.[2] This concept was difficult to understand and apply, but, in general terms, it said that if the agency had limited its discretion to make the decision by saying it could only act when it found that certain facts or conditions existed, a liberty interest had been created, and the decision had to be accompanied by limited due process protections. Under this test, the seriousness of the loss was not a relevant consideration in deciding if due process applied or not—only the language of the rule or policy governing the decision was important.

In *Hewitt*, the Court said that the due process clause did not inherently apply to the decision to place an inmate in administrative segregation. Applying its language-focused test for "state created liberty interests," the Court held that Pennsylvania rules did create a liberty interest. The decision to place an inmate in administrative segregation had to be accompanied by minimal procedural protections, including giving notice to the inmate of the proposed decision and giving the inmate an opportunity to respond, either orally or in writing.

Because the test from *Hewitt* looked only at the language of a rule, and not at the seriousness of the loss the inmate suffered, litigation over very trivial types of decisions was not uncommon. For instance, in one case, the inmate claimed a due process interest in receiving a tray lunch rather than a sack lunch. He won at the district court level, but lost when the case got to the court of appeals.[3]

Thirteen years after it had adopted the language-focused test, the Supreme Court abandoned it. In *Sandin v. Conner*,[4] the court decided that the language-oriented test had become a disincentive to officials wanting to write rules or policies governing various types of decisions. Consider the decision to place an inmate in administrative segregation. Under the language-oriented test, if officials adopted no restricting or controlling rules concerning what would permit an inmate to be placed in administrative segregation, no due process protections would apply. However, if the officials adopted rules (such as saying "an inmate may be placed in administrative segregation only under the following circumstances . . ."), due process protections could arise. Adopting a rule could mean officials increase their liability exposure. The Court also felt the old rule brought federal courts too much into the day-to-day decision making in prisons and jails. The Court cited the sack lunch case mentioned previously as an example.

The Court replaced the old test with a different one. Now, a liberty interest will be created only if the decision results in an "atypical and significant deprivation in relation to the normal incidents of prison life." As with many new legal tests which come from the Supreme Court, it is not clear what an "atypical and significant deprivation" is. We know from the *Sandin* decision that thirty days in disciplinary segregation is not such a deprivation. Lower court decisions, which have interpreted the phrase, tell us that much longer periods in disciplinary segregation also are not so substantial as to trigger due process protections.

Under the "atypical" test, the decision to place an inmate in administrative segregation probably will not be protected by due process. Despite uncertainties about the meaning of the new rule, in general, it should result in fewer court decisions mandating decisions be accompanied with due process protections.

In *Sandin*, the Court said that decisions that adversely affected an inmate's release date remained protected by due process. The Court also said that placement in disciplinary segregation for thirty days did not. However, that left open the question of whether there were other types of decisions adversely affecting inmates that fell between thirty days in disciplinary segregation and changes to a release date that were so serious as to result in "an atypical and significant deprivation" that required due process protections?

The answer to the question was "yes:" At least in some circumstances, the decision to place inmates in ultra-high custody prisons or housing units intended for extended periods of time perhaps running into years resulted in an atypical deprivation.[5] These prisons, called "special housing units" or "extended control units" or in common parlance, "supermaxes," are a sort of administrative segregation unit on steroids. While an administrative segregation unit may hold inmates for weeks or even months, it often may hold an inmate for a relatively short period of time. By contrast, the special housing unit is designed to hold inmates for a very long time in the highest level of security. Inmates will remain in their cells twenty-three hours a day, typically have no face–to-face contact with other inmates, and relatively little face-to-face contact with officers or other staff. As the inmate's behavior and attitude progress, the very strict conditions may be gradually eased and the inmate may move through a series of steps to the point where he or she can be returned to a more traditional prison.

After the Supreme Court announced its "atypical deprivation" test in the *Sandin* case in 1995, many inmates in special housing units sued, arguing that (1) placement in a special housing unit amounted to an atypical and significant deprivation that entitled them to due process protections and (2) the placement process used failed to afford adequate protections.

At least at a superficial level, this was an appealing argument. Placement in a special housing unit for a stay that would be, for instance, eighteen months at a minimum, certainly seemed "atypical" compared to housing in a prison's general population. In many respects, it probably visited a greater loss on the inmate than the loss of fifteen days good time, particularly if the inmate were serving a very long prison term.

In *Wilkinson*, the Supreme Court found that based on the facts of the case before it, placement in Ohio's long-term segregation unit imposed an atypical deprivation. Three factors were important: (1) the placement was for an indefinite period, (2) the conditions in the unit were very restrictive, and (3) placement made the inmate ineligible for parole consideration. If one or two of these conditions were taken away, would the placement still be an atypical deprivation? The Court implied it might not, but offered little guidance on this point.

Having found due process protections were necessary, the Court found that the procedural protections that Ohio provided, which were less stringent than those required for a disciplinary hearings (see below), were sufficient. Ohio gave the inmate facing placement a notice of the factual basis for the proposed decision and an opportunity for rebuttal. The inmate could also offer objections to the initial placement recommendation that would be considered by the final decision makers. Ohio provided a short statement of reasons for the placement and reviewed the initial placement after thirty days. The process did not allow the inmate to call or cross examine witnesses, which the Court said was acceptable. All in all, the procedures followed by Ohio and approved by the Supreme Court did not create an onerous burden on the classification process and, indeed, are consistent with good administrative practice.

Due Process and the Disciplinary Process

Over the years, the main area where procedural due process has been important in prisons or jails is in the disciplinary process. Discipline is vital to preserving security and safety in a correctional facility. If inmates are not held accountable for following certain basic rules of behavior, chaos could result. So, the institution has a strong interest in being able to enforce disciplinary rules quickly and effectively.

On the other side of the balance, inmates have an interest in not being punished for rule violations they did not commit. Violation of an institution rule can carry serious consequences for an inmate, including losing the level of freedom and privileges associated with being in an institution's general population or in a particular custody level in exchange for segregation. A rule violation may affect directly an inmate's release date if it results in a loss of or denial of good time. So, inmates may have certain "liberty interests" at stake in the disciplinary process.

Due Process Applied

In 1974, the Supreme Court was asked to balance the competing interests of the institution and of inmates and to decide if due process protections applied to prison (or jail) disciplinary processes and, if due process did apply, specifically what sort of procedures were necessary.

In *Wolff v. McDonnell*,[6] the Court ruled that where state law created a right to good time and that where good time could be forfeited only for serious misbehavior, some due process protections were necessary "to ensure that the state-created right is not arbitrarily abrogated."

In *Wolff*, the Court also decided what sort of procedural protections the state had to provide in the disciplinary process. Where loss of good time (a serious sanction) was potentially involved, the hearing process had to include the following elements:

- A *hearing* at which the inmate has the right to be present. The inmate can, by words or his or her behavior, waive the right to be present at the hearing.

- *Advance written notice* of the charges, given to the inmate at least twenty-four hours in advance of the hearing. More than twenty-four hours could be required if the facts and circumstances of a particular case were such that twenty-four hours was not enough time for the inmate to prepare for the hearing. The notice should include details about the time and place of the alleged incident and some other details about what the officer preparing the infraction believes occurred. This detail is necessary to allow the inmate a reasonable opportunity to know what he or she is charged with doing so that a defense can be prepared.

- *The opportunity for the* inmate to *call witnesses and present evidence* on his or her own behalf, except when it can be shown that to allow this would, in the Supreme Court's words, "be unduly hazardous to constitutional safety or correctional goals." Where the inmate requests that a particular witness be called and that request is denied, it will be the institution's burden to justify the denial later, if the inmate sues about the denial. Therefore, it becomes important that some sort of record be made of the reasons for a denial. Facility disciplinary rules normally will provide more detail regarding what may justify denying a witness.

- *Assistance*—sometimes. Inmates do not, under any circumstances, have a right to a lawyer in a disciplinary hearing, even if criminal charges may be pending against the inmate.[7] However, under some circumstances, they have a right to assistance. Where the inmate is illiterate or where the complexity of the issues makes it unlikely that the inmate will be able to collect and present the evidence necessary for an adequate comprehension of the case, the inmate is entitled to be assisted by someone. This assistant may be another inmate, a staff member, or other person. The institution largely can control who serves as assistants and can choose, for instance, not to allow inmates to serve in this role.

  The precise role of the assistant will vary depending on the reasons that led to the appointment of the assistant in the first place. Thus, if an assistant is appointed to help an inmate simply because the inmate cannot read, the role may be limited to reading various documents to the inmate. Yet, if the assistant is appointed because the inmate is intellectually not able to understand the hearing process and the issues involved, then the assistant may have to take much more responsibility for investigating and presenting the entire case for the inmate.

  There may be a duty to appoint an assistant in some cases, even where the inmate does not ask for help, since some of the reasons an assistant is needed also might be the reasons why the inmate did not ask for assistance. The hearing officer should be alert to the possible need for assistants in cases and should appoint them where he or she feels there may be a question about the inmate's ability to present his or her own case.

- *Impartial tribunal.* The hearing officer or board must be impartial. If someone is a victim in or a witness to the incident that led to the infraction being charged (or involved with its investigation), the person may not serve as a hearing officer in that hearing. Similarly, if a hearing officer has some personal bias for or against an inmate, he or she should step down. The fact that an inmate has filed a lawsuit against a hearing officer does not require automatic disqualification, but under some circumstances, a lawsuit could raise questions about a hearing officer's impartiality. This would depend on such things as the specific issues in the suit (Were they a direct attack on the officer's discretion? Were they quite personal?) and perhaps the result of the suit, if it had come to an end (Was the officer found liable?).

  The fact that a hearing officer may have heard about an incident prior to the hearing (something that is almost inevitable with serious incidents, particularly in smaller facilities) does not disqualify the person. However, the decision obviously must be based only on the information presented at the hearing, not institution scuttlebutt picked up over coffee.

- *Written decision.* There must be a written statement by the faultfinder (the hearing officer or committee) "as to the evidence relied on and reasons" for the decision. By writing down what evidence the hearing officer believed to be true and indicating why one sanction was selected out of the typical range of sanctions, other agencies or officials (such as paroling authorities or classification committees) can understand the violation better and are less likely to make incorrect decisions about the offender based on a misunderstanding of the infraction. A written statement also allows others to review the decision for its correctness. These "others" might include supervisors within the institution or agency, as well as the court.

A written decision that simply indicates the inmate was guilty or "guilty based on all the evidence" often will not be acceptable. If the evidence was conflicting, as is the case when the officer says the inmate committed the infraction but the inmate and perhaps the inmate's witnesses say the inmate did not, guilty cannot be based on "all the evidence." [8] Obviously, the hearing officer believed some of the evidence and did not believe some. The written decision simply should review what the officer believed to be true.

Courts have not said that inmates have a constitutional right to appeal the result of a disciplinary hearing, but virtually every disciplinary process includes a right to appeal. Appeals give the institution the opportunity to correct possible constitutional errors in a hearing.

When Do *Wolff* Requirements Apply?

Language in the *Wolff* opinion indicated that the Court intended its holding to apply not only when a disciplinary hearing could result in good time being taken away from an inmate, but also when the inmate faced a term in segregation. Virtually all prisons and jails in the country interpreted the case in this way.

In the 1995 decision, *Sandin v. Conner*, the Court indicated that it no longer felt that the requirements of *Wolff* or, indeed, any lesser due process requirements, applied to a disciplinary hearing, which resulted in a thirty-day segregation sanction.[9] The *Sandin* decision does not indicate whether a longer disciplinary segregation penalty might require some due process requirements. Courts consistently have applied the *Sandin* result to exempt segregation sanctions considerably longer than thirty days from due process review, but some courts have suggested that a long enough sanction—perhaps over a year—still would require a full "*Wolff* hearing."[10]

Early cases following *Sandin* left a question of whether full *Wolff* protections still applied to pretrial detainees facing disciplinary proceedings involving a short segregation sanction. While this issue has not been litigated often, most courts have held that Sandin applies only to sentenced offenders and that the traditional *Wolff v. McDonnell* type disciplinary hearing must be given to pretrial detainees.[10]

Wolff asked what form of due process, if any, was required for minor infractions. *Sandin* answers this question by saying that unless a disciplinary sanction imposes an "atypical and significant deprivation (on the inmate) in relation to the normal incidents of prison life," no due process protections are required. *Sandin*, therefore, leaves agencies to address the question of what disciplinary procedures they wish to follow not only for very minor infractions, but also for more serious ones that may carry a maximum penalty of some time in segregation, but which do not directly affect an inmate's release date.

No Right to Counsel or to Confront or Cross-Examine

The Court in *Wolff* refused to allow the inmate the right to confront or cross-examine witnesses against him or her. In general, the Court felt that cross-examination would tend to make the hearings longer and more difficult to manage. In particular, the Court was concerned that requiring cross-examination of inmate informants either would put those persons in serious danger or simply cut off inmates as a source of information.

Wolff also said that inmates do not have a right to counsel (a lawyer) in a disciplinary hearing, even though circumstances may require they be given some type of assistance. The Court re-emphasized its "no-right-to-counsel" holding two years after *Wolff* by reversing a lower court decision that said where the inmate was facing disciplinary charges that involved conduct punishable under a state's criminal code, the inmate still had a right to counsel. The Supreme Court said even under these circumstances, there was no right to a lawyer.

In refusing to impose a right to counsel or a right to cross-examine witnesses, the Supreme Court left two of the most traditional components of due process off the list of procedural rights that must be given to inmates in disciplinary hearings. The Court did this because of the unique problems associated with running a jail or prison disciplinary system. The Court felt the balance tipped strongly in favor of the institution in the right to counsel and the right to cross-examine witnesses, despite their historic part in what has been perceived of as a "fair" hearing.

Inmate Silence

The Fifth Amendment right against self-incrimination does not apply in disciplinary hearings. Thus, if an inmate refuses to testify, the inmate's silence can be used as an indicator of guilt. However, silence alone cannot prove guilt.[11]

Confidential Informants

By refusing to require that inmates in disciplinary hearings be allowed to confront and cross-examine persons testifying against them, the Supreme Court opened the door for the use of information in hearings from anonymous informants. It is literally possible for an inmate to be charged and found guilty in a disciplinary hearing without knowing virtually any of the details of the charge, the source of the charge, and without hearing any direct testimony about the violation.

The ability to consider information from anonymous informants and to withhold both the name of the informant and the detail of the information (when revealing that detail would identify its source) carries with it the serious possibility of abuse. One inmate with a grudge against another may make up a story about a rule violation. Rumor about an inmate's guilt may become fact in a hearing when a charged inmate has no way to rebut the "evidence" since he or she may not even know what the evidence is.

However informant information may be almost the only way information from inmates can be used in hearings, since inmates seldom tolerate "snitches," and the inmate who testifies openly against another places himself or herself in serious danger. If little or no inmate information could be used in hearings, the disciplinary process could be seriously damaged, since many rule violations are not witnessed by staff, but may be witnessed only by inmates.

In an attempt to strike a balance between the potential for abuse from informant testimony and the institution's need to be able to consider information from inmates in the disciplinary process, courts have imposed limitations on how and when informant information may be used. The weight of these limitations falls primarily on hearing officers, but also indirectly on other staff who may bring informant information to the hearing. Unless the information is presented properly, it may not be considered. If it is considered improperly, a court is likely to overturn the results of the hearing and also may impose damages against the hearing officer or others involved in the hearing process and may impose additional requirements, making it even more difficult to consider informant information.

There are two basic requirements that must be met for informant information to be properly considered.[12]

1. **Reliability.** The hearing officer must be convinced the informant is reliable. An officer coming to the hearing and stating "I have information from a reliable informant that . . ." is not enough, because this shows only the officer's conclusion about reliability. The officer must be prepared to explain to the hearing officer (out of the presence of the charged inmate) why the source is a reliable one. Then, when the hearing officer has facts, not just conclusions, to consider, he or she can decide if the informant is reliable.

   Where the hearing officer is convinced the informant is generally reliable, the specific information can be considered, and the second requirement arises.

2. **Credibility.** Assuming the informant is generally reliable, the next question is whether the specific information offered is believable enough to prove, or help prove, guilt. If the informant information is corroborated by other evidence in the hearing, it gains credibility. The more detailed the information is, the more credible it becomes. Unless the informant was an eyewitness to the incident, the information is suspect. Normally hearsay information ("Well, I didn't see the assault, but another inmate who did told me it happened this way.") should not be considered. An exception to this rule might be where the hearsay is actually an admission by the charged inmate ("Well, I didn't see the incident, but the charged inmate told me he did it.") Again, the hearing officer is the one who must be convinced that the information is credible.

Sometimes, the reliability and credibility determinations will blend together, but generally, the hearing officer must decide if the information is or is not believable both in light of the nature of the information itself and its source.

Evidence and the Reporting Officer

Due process allows federal courts to review the sufficiency of the evidence in a disciplinary hearing, but only in a very limited way. Where the record of a hearing shows there was "some evidence" on which the hearing officer could have relied in making a finding of guilt, due process is satisfied. The reviewing judge is not allowed to second-guess the hearing officer. Even if the judge would not have found guilt on the basis of the evidence, if there is "some evidence," the decision must stand.[13] State law may permit state courts to review the sufficiency of the evidence more closely.

A continuing issue with disciplinary hearings is whether the reporting officer should, or must, be present to testify. Courts have not given a clear, absolute ruling on this issue. In general, the more complicated the issues in the hearing, the more important it is for the officer to testify in person. Where the factual questions in the hearing are quite simple (as is often the case), and where the officer has written a clear, complete report to support the charge, the officer's presence is less important.

Basing a finding of guilt just on a poorly written report, where the inmate presents a plausible defense that the report may not directly respond to (such as mistaken identity or facts not addressed in the report) invites court intervention in the disciplinary process.

Making a Record

It is unlikely a hearing decision will be overturned because it fails to meet the "some evidence" test. What is more likely is that a decision may be overturned because the record (which is usually all the reviewing court has to consider) is not clear or detailed enough to allow the court to tell what evidence the hearing officer relied on or what the basis was for key decisions, such as denial of a witnesses' request.

"The record" consists of all the paperwork generated by a hearing and any tape recording (or written transcript) of the hearing itself. If something is not "in the record," a court may assume it did not happen. For example, in one case an inmate was charged with possession of marijuana. The evidence consisted of a bag of what was identified as marijuana, which was found in the pocket of a shirt hanging in the inmate's cell. The hearing and the subsequent lawsuit focused largely on how the material in the bag could be identified as marijuana. (Could an officer identify it based on his experience and training, or must a chemical test of some sort be done?) While the court said the officer's identification was sufficient, the court threw out the hearing because the record failed to show that anyone identified the bag of marijuana as the bag found in the inmate's shirt.[14] A trivial oversight? Probably so. Nevertheless, it was fatal to the hearing.

Where tape recordings of the hearings are not available (either because tapes were not made or were destroyed before the suit challenging the hearing result was filed), the court is limited to considering the written record, especially the written decision made by the hearing officer. The record will be the basis of not only a court review of the sufficiency of the evidence, but also of virtually every other discretionary decision the hearing officer makes that is of legal significance: Was there a sufficient reason to deny a witness?[15] Was the informant reliable and credible? Should an assistant have been appointed? A hearing that, in fact, met all the procedural requirements, correctly decided the inmate was guilty, and imposed an appropriate sanction can be thrown out unless the record is sufficient to establish those facts.

Remember that there probably are more decisions made that have potential constitutional importance in disciplinary hearings than in any other part of prison or jail operation. However, these decisions almost all deal with procedural questions—"technicalities" to many who work in the institution. To institution staff, the important part of a disciplinary hearing is the result: Is the inmate guilty and, if so, what penalty should be imposed? Nevertheless, a court will be concerned about the procedural issues and the quality of the record—the "technicalities." So, unless the institution can demonstrate, almost always through the hearing record, that the procedural requirements were met, the hearing result may be a lost case.

Involuntary Medication

An inmate is diagnosed as mentally ill. Mental health experts feel the inmate may be dangerous to himself or others. Line staff who must deal with the inmate reach similar conclusions, based on watching the inmate's behavior.

According to the psychiatrist, the best course of treatment is for the inmate to take what is known as an antipsychotic medication. However, the inmate refuses to take such medication. He claims these drugs can produce serious—sometimes permanent—side effects and they make him feel "strange."

Outside the institution, people have a right to refuse treatment, including treatment for mental illness. Yet, the state can overcome that right in certain circumstances and can put the person in a mental hospital and involuntarily medicate the person. Because civil commitment takes away a person's liberty and because of the seriousness of involuntarily medicating someone, due process requires that the decision to commit and medicate individuals against their will be approved by a court.

In early 1990, the Supreme Court looked at the question of whether similar due process protections were necessary to involuntarily medicate a mentally ill inmate in *Washington v. Harper*. The Court said a judicial hearing was not needed, but also said that "We have no doubt that (the inmate) possesses a significant liberty interest in avoiding the unwanted administration of antipsychotic drugs under the due process clause of the Fourteenth Amendment."[16] Having decided that the decision to involuntarily medicate the inmate was protected by due process, the Court then indicated what sorts of circumstances would permit medicating the inmate and approved the procedures being followed by the State of Washington, where the case arose.

A person with a serious mental illness and who was dangerous to himself or herself or others may be medicated, when the treatment is in the inmate's medical interest, said the Court. The Court approved a hearing process for making these determinations, which somewhat resembled an inmate-disciplinary hearing, although it included some greater procedural protections (the right to cross-examine witnesses, the right to be assisted by someone who understood the psychiatric issues involved, and a three-person hearing panel that included mental health experts). In 1992, the Supreme Court said that in certain circumstances pretrial detainees also could be involuntarily medicated.[17]

Substantive Due Process

In some situations, the focus of due process is on what is done, not just how it is done, which is the concern of procedural due process. Where the substance of the decision is the key issue, substantive due process or "fundamental fairness" will be the basis for the court's analysis. Under this approach, a court in essence may say, "It makes no difference how many procedural protections might accompany the decision or facts in question—what the government is doing simply should not be allowed, period."

The involuntary medication decision, *Washington v. Harper*, included a substantive due process component when the Court ruled on what sorts of circumstances had to exist to justify involuntarily medicating an inmate. Unless the inmate was dangerous to himself or others and involuntary treatment was in the inmate's medical interest, the inmate could not be involuntarily medicated, regardless of how many procedures the institution might go through.

However, the main area in corrections where substantive due process is important is in litigation regarding the conditions of confinement of pretrial detainees. The Eighth Amendment's prohibition of cruel and unusual punishment regulates conditions of confinement for convicted persons. Yet, the Eighth Amendment does not protect persons before they are convicted, such as pretrial detainees. To assure that conditions of confinement are at least no worse for pretrial detainees than for convicted persons, the courts review and regulate detainees' conditions of confinement under substantive due process. The end result is essentially the same: there is no clear difference between what conditions must exist for convicted persons (Eighth Amendment analysis) and for pretrial detainees (Fourteenth Amendment, substantive due process analysis). The difference really is only what legal route the court takes to the final result.

Substantive due process also may be the basis for a court reviewing allegations of excess force made by pretrial detainees.

Equal Protection

It is sometimes said that equal protection outlaws discrimination between people or groups. This overstates the meaning of equal protection. The concept of equal protection says that groups of persons that are generally similar to one another should be treated the same by the government, unless the government can justify treating them differently.

The strength of the government's justification may have to be greater or lesser, depending on the groups and the reason for the discrimination between them. For instance, if discrimination on the basis of race (a so-called "suspect" classification) is shown (such as segregated cellblocks), the government must demonstrate a "compelling" need for the segregation. This is a very difficult burden to meet, so racial discrimination is almost never constitutionally justified. Conscious decisions to discriminate on the basis of race are probably relatively rare. More likely, discrimination and resulting segregation of racial groups could occur as an unintentional consequence of applying a classification system.

Distinctions based on gender can be justified if they serve important government objectives and are substantially related to those objectives. This is a somewhat easier burden to meet than that for racial discrimination.

Racial Segregation

Case Study: White Segregation

White inmates at the Pontiac Correctional Center in Illinois sued. They claimed the large percentage of white inmates in protective custody violated their equal protection rights to be free from racial segregation. Although whites made up only 12 percent of the total institution population, 40 percent of the white population was in protective custody. The plaintiffs claimed this was the result of the administration being too tolerant of gangs (which were virtually all either black or Hispanic).

The court rejected the claim, saying that unless the plaintiffs could show intentional discrimination by the administration, their equal protection claim must fail. Despite its legal conclusion, the court was very critical of the gang policies of the administration, which the court believed had led to a very serious problem, even though it did not violate the equal protection clause. *David K. v. Lane*, 839 F.2d 1265 (7th Cir., 1988).

Over the last sixty years, the most important equal protection issue the courts have addressed is that of discrimination on the basis of race. One of the earliest corrections cases decided by the Supreme Court found a policy of racial segregation in prisons to be unconstitutional.[18] Alabama officials argued that the lower court's order to desegregate the state's prisons did not leave room for considerations of prison security and discipline, but the majority rejected this reading of the lower court's order. Three justices concurred but added that in certain circumstances, prison officials could take racial tensions into consideration.

A decision from 1968 seems like old news in a publication printed more than four decades later. However, the Supreme Court revisited racial segregation in prison in a case 2004 from California and reiterated the principle that to justify racial discrimination in a prison setting, officials have the same, very difficult legal burden that applies to any other form of government discrimination based on race.[19]

The California Department of Corrections segregated male inmates by race for up to two months every time they entered a new prison. The Department argued the measure was necessary to prevent gang violence. The Supreme Court took the case to decide what the legal test for evaluating racial segregation in the prison setting should be. The Ninth Circuit had approved the policy, using the legal test from *Turner v. Safley*, 482 U.S. 78 (1987), which asks only if there is a rational basis for the action of prison officials. The Supreme Court reversed, saying that even though the matter came out of the prison context, the proper legal test was the traditional test for racial discrimination under the Equal Protection Clause, in other words, "strict scrutiny." The strict scrutiny test does not say that racial discrimination in prison can never be justified, but to justify it, officials must show that their actions further a "compelling governmental interest" (such as prison security) in a way that is "narrowly tailored to address those necessities."[20]

The Supreme Court remanded the case back to the lower courts to analyze the facts under the proper legal test. Subsequently, the parties mediated a settlement under which the Department has removed race as a primary deciding factor in housing decisions.

The message from the *Johnson* case is that a formal or informal policy of segregating inmates on the basis of race remains very difficult, if not impossible to legally justify. However, racial tensions can be taken into consideration in more specific, focused situations.

Male versus Female Facilities and Programs

During the 1980s and early 1990s, some courts found that the equal protection clause required "parity" between the programs and facilities provided to men and women. That which was provided to women had to be "substantially equivalent to (that which was) provided to men, in other words, equivalent in substance if not form." However, in the mid 1990s, courts of appeal cases rejected the type of equal protection comparisons lower courts had used in the so-called "parity" cases and the parity idea largely ended.

Review Questions

1. Why are there more procedural rights in a parole-revocation hearing than in a prison or jail disciplinary hearing?

2. What is the difference between procedural and substantive due process, and where might each arise in a prison or jail setting?

3. Under what circumstances may a hearing officer rely on evidence from a witness whose identity is not disclosed to the inmate charged with the offense?

[21.] *Klinger v. Department of Corrections*, 31 F.3d 727, 737 (8th Cir., 1994); *Women Prisoners of the District of Columbia Department of Corrections*, 93 F.3d 910 (D.C. Cir., 1996).

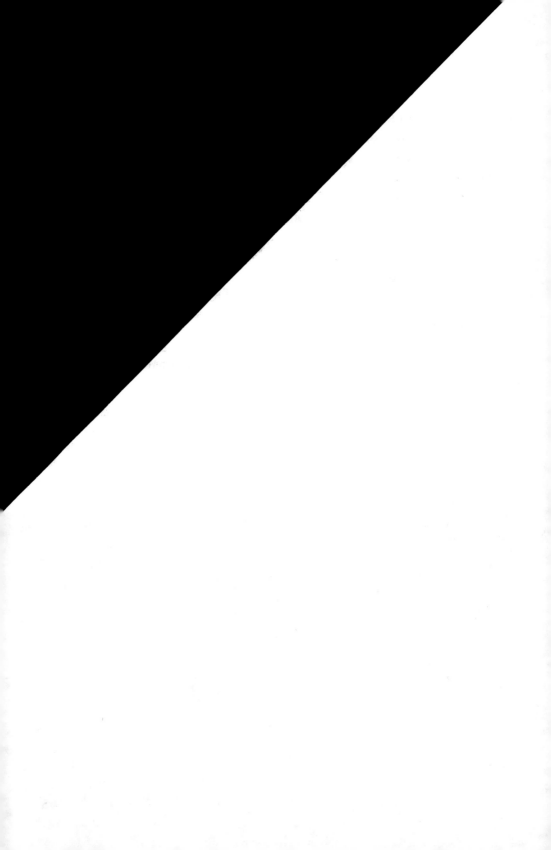

Endnotes

1. *Washington v. Harper*, 494 U.S. 210 (1990).

2. *Hewitt v. Helms*, 459 U.S. 460 (1983).

3. *Burgin v. Nix*, 899 F.2d 733 (8th Circuit 1990).

4. *Sandin v. Conner*, 115 S.Ct. 2293 (1995).

5. *Wilkinson v. Austin*, 545 U.S. 174 (2005).

6. *Wolff v. McDonnell; Baxter v. Palmigiano*, 425 U.S. 308 (1976).

7. *Redding v. Fairman*, 717 F.2d 1105 (7th Cir., 1983).

8. *Sandin v. Conner*, 115 S.Ct. 2293 (1995).

9. *Whitford v. Boglino*, 63 F.3d 527 (7th Cir. 1995).

10. *Fuentes v. Wagner*, 206 F.3d 335 (3rd Cir., 2000); *Rapier v. Harris*, 172 F. 3d 999 (7th Cir., 1999); *Mitchell v. Dupnik*, 75 F.3d 517 (9th Cir. 1996).

11. *Baxter v. Palmigiano*, 425 U.S. 308 (1976).

12. *Baxter v. Palmigiano.*

13. *Wells v. Israel*, 629 F.Supp. 498 (E.D. Wisc., 1986); *McCollum v. Williford*, 793 F.2d 903 (7th Cir., 1986).

14. *Superintendent v. Hill*, 105 S.Ct. 2768 (1985).

15. In re Reismiller, 678 P.2d 323 (Wash., 1984).

16. *Washington v. Harper*, 110 S.Ct. 1028 (1990).

17. *Riggins v. Nevada*, 112 S.Ct. 1810 (1992).

18. *Lee v. Washington*, 390 U.S. 333 (1968).

19. *Johnson v. California*, 543 U.S. 499 (2005).

20. 543 U.S. at 512.

21. *Klinger v. Department of Corrections*, 31 F.3d 727, 737 (8th Cir., 1994); *Women Prisoners of the District of Columbia Department of Corrections*, 93 F.3d 910 (D.C. Cir., 1996).

Chapter 12:
The Correctional Employee and Litigation:
How a Lawsuit Works

Being sued is, unfortunately, an occupational hazard for persons working in corrections. While attorneys who defend these cases are familiar with how litigation "works," the defendant-employee often is not. This unfamiliarity may increase the anxiety attached to being sued. This chapter explains some of the mechanics of litigation, in the hopes that by understanding better the employee's litigation-related anxiety may be minimized.

Lawyers who defend suits are very familiar with the way suits wind their way from summons and complaint, through discovery and pretrial motions, to trial, appeal, and final decision. Unfortunately, due to the press of work and because of their own uncertainty about what will happen next, the lawyer may forget to keep the client advised of progress of the suit or even if the case has been dismissed. (The overwhelming majority of cases filed directly by inmates are resolved in favor of defendants.)

The correctional employee who is a defendant in a suit should have no hesitation in asking his or her lawyer about the status of a case. It is the lawyer's obligation to keep the client advised of this information. So, if in doubt, ask.

Indemnification of Government Employees in Civil Actions

Among the first concerns of an employee working in a profession where lawsuits are so common often is, "Will I have to pay damages? Will I have to pay for my attorney?" The answer to these questions is generally "no."

State Employees

Virtually every state in the country, by statutes often known as tort claims acts, has a procedure by which state employees sued in the line of work are (1) defended by the state attorney general and (2) indemnified for any costs of litigation, including attorneys' fees and damages. Even when a judgment may indicate it is against the defendant "personally," the state typically pays the judgment.

These defense/indemnification statutes act much like a private insurance policy for the employee. However, like many insurance policies, they are not absolute. While the exceptions vary from state to state, in general, the tort claims acts provide that the state is not under a duty to defend if the actions of the employee were outside the scope of the employee's duties or were not taken in good faith.

Thus, in one situation, a state refused to defend an employee of a women's prison in a suit that alleged he had fathered a child of the plaintiff, which was conceived and born while the woman was in the institution. After blood tests determined a very strong probability that the defendant had fathered the child, the state withdrew its defense since there was no way impregnating an inmate could be seen as being within the duties of the defendant-officer.

Employees are wise to determine what exceptions or limitations may exist in defense/indemnification statutes in their jurisdiction and to determine if their state gives a broad or a narrow interpretation to what sort of actions may be within the "scope of employment." If the phrase is given a narrow, conservative interpretation, fewer suits against employees will be defended than if the phrase is given a broad interpretation.

Employees of Local Government

It is a little more difficult to generalize about the protections employees of local government enjoy in this area. Some states may have "little tort claims acts" that provide protection similar to that enjoyed by state employees. Other jurisdictions may carry insurance or self-insure. As with state employees, persons working for local government should determine the scope of protection they have from whatever insurance or statutory defense/indemnification procedure may exist in their jurisdiction.

Suits are serious matters and cannot be ignored by an employee named as a defendant. However, the employee should not be greatly concerned that he or she will incur out-of-pocket expenses in defending the suit or in paying any judgment that the plaintiff might obtain.

168

Criminal Actions

In rare cases, criminal actions may be brought against government employees, either by state or federal prosecuting authorities. Defense of these actions by government attorneys, like defense of civil actions, also usually will depend on specific statutory authority. If such authority exists, it usually will be more restrictive than that for tort claims acts. In other words, there would be fewer situations in which the government could defend its employee in a job-related criminal action.

Summons and Complaint: The Beginnings of a Lawsuit

Generally speaking, the first notification a defendant has that a suit has been filed against him or her is with the receipt of two documents known as a *summons* and a *complaint*. The summons officially notifies the defendant that a suit has been filed and that the defendant has a limited period of time (usually twenty or thirty days) in which to respond to ("answer") the allegations of the complaint. The complaint indicates who the plaintiff and defendant are and states what the plaintiff alleges the defendant did or did not do, how that action or inaction violates the rights of the plaintiff, and what relief the plaintiff seeks.

Different courts have different means of "serving" a summons and complaint on a defendant. In some cases, the documents may be served by any disinterested person. Federal courts often require that a federal marshal serve the documents, although in some cases, service by certified mail is allowed. Generally, service by regular mail will not be considered effective, since the plaintiff ultimately may have to prove the summons and complaint were served on the defendant.

Employees should not attempt to decide whether service of documents that appear to be a summons and complaint (or other litigation-related documents) is good or not, but, instead, should notify their attorneys (or at least supervisors) immediately of the receipt of the documents. Prompt response to a summons and a complaint is necessary. Unless a formal answer or other appropriate documents are filed on behalf of the defendant within the time specified in the summons, a plaintiff, by proving the documents were served on the defendant, can obtain what is called a *default judgment* from the court. This judgment will award the plaintiff all, or at least a substantial part, of what the complaint asks for without any participation of the defendant whatsoever.

One thing a defendant served with a summons and a complaint should not do is answer the allegations personally by directly contacting either the plaintiff or the plaintiff's lawyer. The "answer" called for by the summons is a formal document that, unless properly prepared, may inadvertently hurt the defendant's defense of the suit in some way. The proper response to a summons and a complaint is for the defendant to contact his or her attorney. Agencies should have policies that address how an employee should notify the agency lawyer when served with a summons and a complaint.

What Next? Just the Facts

The lawyer defending the case will need to get the defendant's version of what happened soon after the complaint is served to be able to file an answer and to begin putting the defense of the case together. It is vital that the lawyer be advised of all the relevant facts surrounding the allegations. It is common for a complaint to allege facts that tend to support the claim of the lawsuit and to ignore or overlook facts not favorable to the plaintiff's position. Unless the defendant's lawyer is made aware of these facts, the case may be lost.

Sometimes a defendant will not tell the lawyer of certain facts because the defendant feels that they are not important or because they may be embarrassing to the individual. Again, withholding facts from the lawyer for these sorts of reasons can create very serious problems in the defense of the case.

Discovery

Under the rules by which suits operate (rules of civil procedure), each side is entitled to attempt to find out virtually all of the facts possessed by the other side prior to the time the case goes to trial. This process is called *discovery*. The theory behind discovery is that cases will be settled more readily and justice will be served better when each side knows virtually all of the facts relevant to the suit. This is better than having the suit determined by surprise, when one side manages to hide key facts from the other until the trial is underway.

Discovery takes four primary forms: depositions, interrogatories, motions to produce documents, and requests for admissions. We will look at each of these.

Depositions

A deposition involves a lawyer for one side in a case examining a witness for the other side. The testimony is given under oath before a court reporter, but without a judge being present. Depositions of plaintiff and defendants in suits are very common, and lawyers generally will attempt to depose any and all witnesses who the other side proposes to call at trial or other people who the lawyer feels may have information important to the case.

Interrogatories

Interrogatories are written questions from one side to the other, which the party is required to answer under oath. Interrogatories (often accompanied by requests for admissions to specific facts) generally look for fairly objective sorts of information, including such basic information as who the witnesses in a case may be.

Motions to Produce

These are requests that the party produce documents in his or her possession that may be relevant to the suit. Motions to produce documents often accompany interrogatories. The interrogatory will ask the party to identify what documents may exist relevant to the controversy, and the motion to produce will request the identified documents be turned over to the requesting party.

Requests for Admissions

Requests for admissions sometimes are used to determine basic facts in a case. They request the person to whom they are directed to either admit or deny a specific statement. Requests for admissions must be treated with care because the discovery rule that allows them requires that they be answered within a specific time (perhaps as little as twenty days) and provides that, unless a request for admission is denied or formally objected to within that time period, it will be treated as being admitted.

Handling discovery requests involves the cooperation of lawyer and client. The client should respond to discovery requests only through counsel, but the client may have to do the bulk of the work in responding since, for instance, the client (not the lawyer) will know what documents exist, where they are, and so forth.

Trial Avoidance Techniques

Trials often are avoided through an out-of-court settlement of the case. Some cases are dismissed before ever reaching the trial stage. There are two methods commonly used, especially in inmate-filed cases that often result in dismissal of the case in favor of the defendant before trial.

Motions to Dismiss

The first of these is known as a *motion to dismiss* or a Rule 12(b)(6) motion (which refers to the *Rule of Civil Procedure* that allows such motions). In a motion to dismiss, the defendant says, in essence, "Assuming all of the facts alleged by the plaintiff to be true, the plaintiff is still not entitled to any relief because the facts do not show the defendant violated any right of the plaintiff."

As an absurd example, an inmate-plaintiff might allege that his rights were violated because he was not allowed to bring a dozen friends from across the state to the prison at state expense to help him celebrate his birthday. A court would respond to a motion to dismiss in this case by saying, "Even if these facts are true, the state has no legal duty to spend money to help an inmate celebrate his birthday. Therefore, the plaintiff fails to state a claim upon which relief can be granted and the defendant's motion to dismiss is granted. Case dismissed."

Summary Judgment

The second motion frequently used to dispose of cases before trial (and which can be brought by either party) is a motion for *summary judgment*. Here, where a party can show through affidavits and other documents that there are no significant facts at issue between the parties, the moving party is entitled to have the judge decide the case on its legal merits, in other words, grant a "summary" judgment. If there is no dispute about the material facts in a case, then there is no need to have a trial, and the judge can apply the law to the facts that the parties agree exist.

Summary judgments often are used in lawsuits in which the inmate claims that medical care he or she received was inadequate. Affidavits of medical staff and copies of medical records can show what care the inmate actually received. Then, a court often will rule that the care the inmate received clearly showed more than "deliberate indifference to a serious medical need" and grant the defendants' motion for summary judgment.

Trial and Appeal

The trial is the process by which each side presents its case to the "trier of fact" (the judge or the jury) for determination as to whose version of the facts—the plaintiff's or the defendant's—is the more believable. In a jury case, the jury decides "the facts" but is instructed by the judge as to what the law is. The jury then determines if the facts that they have found violate the law as it is described to them.

Testifying

Where there is a trial, there is testimony. Testifying can be a very stressful process for a witness, especially when the witness may have important testimony to offer and is not familiar with the process of testifying from other court appearances.

Prior to going onto the witness stand, the lawyer presenting the witness should discuss the issues that will be covered and the questions to be asked with the witness. There is nothing wrong with this, and, in fact, no good lawyer will put witnesses on the stand without talking to them. (A saying among lawyers is, "Never ask a witness a question unless you know the answer.") If asked by the opposing lawyer, "Have you discussed your testimony with anyone prior to taking the stand?," the witness should not hesitate in saying, "Yes." If asked with whom the testimony was discussed, the witness can readily state it was with his or her lawyer.

There are many lists of suggestions for witnesses. The following list may help the witness present testimony in the best possible way.

1. Be familiar with the subject of your testimony before taking the stand. Review your records and notes. Review depositions you gave, perhaps months before trial.

2. Dress neatly. Act and appear professional the entire time you are at court, not just while you are on the witness stand. If you wear a uniform, check with your lawyer as to whether you should wear the uniform to testify.

3. Arrive early and let your lawyer know you are present. You may have to wait outside the courtroom before testifying.

4. Do not memorize your testimony. Not only will it not sound natural if you forget your "lines," but your testimony will be very unconvincing.

5. When testifying, speak loudly and clearly. Speak so that you can be heard by the farthest juror. And speak. You cannot answer with a nod or shake of the head or a shrug. Your testimony is being transcribed, and the court reporter only can record verbal answers, not body language.

6. Listen to the question. Be sure you understand it before answering, and answer only the question asked. Think about your answer before you give it, and avoid giving snap answers. If you do not understand the question, ask that it be clarified.

7. Do not volunteer additional information. If you feel you have answered the question, stop talking. If the lawyer delays in asking the next question, do not feel obligated to fill the silence with an additional answer.

8. Try to answer questions "yes" or "no" or otherwise with short answers. If the lawyer wants only a yes or no answer and you cannot answer with just a yes or no, say so. You should be allowed to explain your answer.

9. Correct answers that you give in error. It is easier to correct a mistake as it happens than to try to fix it later.

10. Witnesses normally will not be allowed to give opinions. Testify just to the facts, and do not be afraid to say "I do not know" or "I cannot remember." Do not exaggerate or try to make up details in an attempt to make your testimony sound better. Stick to what you know. **TELL THE TRUTH**! Telling the truth, and the whole truth, begins when you first talk to a lawyer.

11. Always be courteous. This may be easier said than done if the lawyer questioning you is hostile, but getting angry with the lawyer or trying to act "smart" with the lawyer usually will work against you.

12. Do not look to the court for help or guidance in answering a question. Your lawyer should object if the question is improper. If no objection is made, you should answer the question. An exception to this is where you are testifying without a lawyer (perhaps introducing records in a dispute between two other parties). In this situation, you may ask the judge about answering, at least to a limited degree.

13. Stop talking when the judge interrupts or an attorney objects to a question. When being cross-examined by the opposing lawyer, it is a good practice to pause for a couple of seconds before beginning your answer to allow your lawyer to make objections.

14. When your testimony is complete, leave the courtroom with a confident expression. Normally, you should not linger in the courtroom (unless you are a party in the case and attending the entire trial).

Trial and Your Lawyer

While to the observer, a trial may seem to be a slow, plodding activity, to the lawyer actually trying the case, the trial is a very intense time. The court expects one witness to be called after another, and the lawyer is expected to be ready to proceed with the case from start to finish without delay. While a witness worries about his or her own testimony, the lawyer may be worrying about testimony and the scheduling of a dozen witnesses, plus a variety of other concerns.

Because of the intensity of the trial and because of the pressure to keep the trial moving, an individual witness may feel he or she is being treated brusquely by the court and even by the lawyer who called the witness. To a large extent, this is simply inevitable, and the witness should not expect to have time to discuss the testimony with the lawyer just before or after the witness is called to testify. However, a good lawyer will make every effort to discuss the testimony with a witness at some time shortly before the witness testifies.

Appeal

On appeal, no further testimony is taken. Instead, the appellate court reviews the written record from the trial and determines if the law was correctly applied. Except in rare cases, the appellate court is bound by the facts found by the original judge or jury, since the appellate court is not able to evaluate the credibility and demeanor of the witnesses who testified at trial.

Conclusion

The correctional employee should remember that, except in truly rare circumstances, lawsuits against an employee do not threaten the employee's personal finances. Additionally, although offenders may file a large number of suits, the overwhelming majority of such suits are resolved in favor of the defendant/correctional employee, usually without even going to trial.

It is equally important to recognize that suits are serious matters and should not be taken lightly. The employee who is sued needs to make prompt contact with legal counsel and work closely with counsel through the defense of the case.

Review Questions

1. Under what circumstances is an agency likely to refuse to defend an employee sued by an inmate?

2. Name two types of discovery.

3. True or False: When testifying, the witness should try to memorize answers to the lawyers' questions.

Chapter 13:
Officers' Rights

Inmates are not the only people to repeatedly turn to the courts to settle disputes in the last quarter of the twentieth century. Americans of every description are becoming quick to file lawsuits. America is a litigious society; Americans file many lawsuits.

Corrections has not escaped being the target of lawsuits from persons other than inmates, and officers may see these suits during their work. In some cases, officers may file such claims and/or be the target of them.

Sources of Officers' Rights

Correctional staff are increasingly sensitive about their rights and the obligations of others toward officers. While inmates usually must look to the Constitution for legal protection, legally enforceable rights of staff come from many sources, not just the Constitution.

Union Contracts

Where a union exists, the labor agreement may create a variety of rights for union members. These can include seniority and job assignments, overall working conditions, procedures to be followed in discipline, grievance procedures, layoffs, and other protections. An employer's ability to implement a urine testing program (which may include random testing) may be limited by the bargaining agreement—the employer may not have the power to begin a urinalysis program without the agreement of the union.

Where collective bargaining between an agency and employees is permitted, it is controlled by state law. The state law will define what subjects are open for collective bargaining and what are not. "Bargainable" issues typically include such things as working conditions and other personnel-related matters.

Workload and safety generally are considered to be mandatory subjects of bargaining. Those issues not subject to bargaining are those that are considered to be managerial.

Unfortunately, the line between subjects that are or are not subject to bargaining often is not clear. Two issues that often are subject to dispute as to whether they are bargainable issues are employee urine testing programs and the decision to make a workplace smoke-free.

Civil Service Laws

Laws and regulations adopted under civil service laws usually define the procedures to be followed in employee discipline proceedings, defining the due process owed the employee facing discipline. Many correctional administrators complain that the often stringent legal requirements created by these laws (and sometimes by union contracts, as well) make it very difficult to discipline an employee.

Discrimination Laws

Statutes and regulations have been adopted at both the federal and state level prohibiting discrimination against a variety of protected groups or categories. Discrimination on the basis of race, sex, national origin, religion, color, age, and handicap generally are prohibited. Discrimination issues may arise in a variety of employment-related contexts, beginning with job advertising and recruiting; and continuing through testing; hiring; making assignments; transferring; promoting; training; disciplining; providing compensation and benefits; terminating; and virtually every other term, condition, and privilege of employment.

Discrimination claims may be brought by specific individuals or by groups claiming they have been systematically discriminated against in some way. In one case, an employer who passed over a woman for a major promotion in a large accounting firm told her she should be "more feminine" in a number of ways. Standing alone, this sort of sexual stereotyping would have violated the law and not been a legitimate ground for denying her a promotion. However, the employer claimed it had other legally permissible reasons for passing over the woman. The Supreme Court said that where first the employee shows that gender was a motivating factor for the decision, the employer still could escape liability by proving by a preponderance of the evidence (a lower "burden of proof" than the lower court had required) that it would have reached the same employment decision ("We would not have promoted her anyway.")[1]

This shows the legal complexity that can arise in a case involving a single person. The complexity multiplies overwhelmingly when a group claims it has been discriminated against. The evidence in such cases seldom will be direct. An employer will not have a written policy that says, "We do not promote women or minorities." The evidence in such cases often is statistical: the number of protected group members in a given employment category is so small it only can be explained by discrimination. The Supreme Court has approved such statistical approaches, saying an inference of discrimination may be drawn through such means, but the comparison (in a promotional case situation) must be between the number of higher level jobs and the numbers of the protected group in the labor market qualified to hold those jobs. The employees also must show a particular employment practice causes a statistical disparity. Where the employees meet these difficult burdens, the employer may defend itself successfully by showing the challenged practice serves legitimate employment goals.[2]

The area of discrimination law becomes even more complicated because most claims arise under laws passed by Congress or state legislatures and later are interpreted by the courts. A court may interpret a law in a way not intended by the legislative body that passed it. This may lead the legislative body to pass amendments to the law to correct what it feels was the court's misapplication of the legislative intent.

Affirmative Action

In a sense, affirmative action programs are the flip side of discrimination laws. The general goal of these programs is to increase the number of protected group members in the workforce. However, unless they are carefully structured and implemented, affirmative action programs can discriminate illegally against other people. A voluntary affirmative action plan that includes goals, not specific quotas, and is designed to attain, not maintain, a balanced workforce, is acceptable if it is attempting to remedy a "manifest imbalance" in a "traditionally segregated job category."[3] The imbalance sought to be corrected need not be the result of actions by the employer, but can be the result of societal pressures and attitudes. Yet, where there is a specific history of an employer discriminating against a protected group, specific hiring quotas may be ordered by a court.[4]

Sexual Discrimination and Harassment

One form of unlawful discrimination warrants special discussion. Sexual discrimination is outlawed by Title VII of the federal Civil Rights Act, 42 USC 2000e. Because increasing numbers of women are entering the workforce in male

179

facilities where the workforce traditionally has been almost all male, sexual discrimination can be a very real problem in such workplaces.

Unless there is a truly legitimate reason for treating persons differently on the basis of their sex (a "bona fide occupational qualification" or BFOQ), discrimination is illegal. The same exception applies to types of generally unlawful discrimination, such as racial discrimination. The BFOQ concept is narrowly defined and applied. One example where it might be applied is to justify a single-sex post in an institution where the post (or a specific task) involves very close scrutiny of inmates in states of undress. In this situation, use of officers of the opposite sex of the inmates may be seen as an invasion of the inmates' privacy rights.

While sexual discrimination may be thought of as only including such things as refusing a person a job because of their sex, the concept also includes sexual harassment. Indeed, it is sexual harassment that may present the most potential conflict in the male prison setting.

To be considered sexual harassment one or more of the following conditions must be met:

1. Submission to the conduct is made (either directly or by inference) a condition of employment or for other employment-related decisions (promotions, working conditions, and so forth). The most flagrant example of this exists where an employer or supervisor tells someone, "If you want this job, you must have sex with me."

2. The conduct has either the purpose or the effect of unreasonably interfering with a person's work performance or creating an intimidating, hostile, or offensive work environment. This is probably the most common area of complaint. (A hostile work environment also can be the basis for a claim of racial discrimination.)

Under the "hostile-work-environment" approach, such things as unwanted touches, comments, or photos (physical, verbal, or visual conduct) may create the basis of a legitimate complaint. Sexual stereotyping (such as asking a female employee to get coffee, take notes, and do other "women's work") also can create a hostile work environment.

In general, the conduct must be unwanted, and the persons who feel offended by the conduct must make it known that they want the conduct to stop. This can add a level of uncertainty because milder forms of potentially sexually harassing conduct may be seen by some as routine and not offensive, but may be very offensive to others.

Employees should receive training on sexual harassment and discrimination issues. The following basic points should be remembered:

1. Sexual harassment is against the law.

2. Sexual harassment suits can be very expensive and time-consuming to defend and can result in liability both against individual staff members and the agency.

3. Sexual harassment suits can be very destructive of employee morale, as one group becomes pitted against another.

4. Inmates will be quick to sense the disruption among staff and try to exploit it.

Rights for Disabled Staff

The Americans with Disabilities Act (ADA) prohibits discrimination against otherwise qualified staff or job applicants on the basis of a disability. The law requires the employer to make "reasonable accommodations" for disabled persons and includes various remedies, including lawsuits for people who feel their rights under the law have been violated. Compliance with the requirements of ADA in the hiring and employment process may require not only various physical changes in buildings, but changes in employment testing, job qualifications, and job structure. The ADA is discussed at greater length in Chapter 14.

Workplace Safety

Workplace safety increasingly involves "legal issues." Here, claims may arise under union contracts, under state or federal occupational safety and health laws, or under the Constitution. In one startling action, correctional officers and their union joined with inmates in 1989 to file a lawsuit against a large metropolitan jail challenging crowding and the alleged lack of workplace safety (argued to be a by-product of the crowding).[5]

Other constitutional claims made by correctional staff about inadequate safety have not done well in court. According to at least two federal appeals courts, the state has no constitutional duty to protect officers. Since such a duty exists for inmates, why not for officers? The courts said it is because the officers are free to leave. The duty to protect applies only to those held in the state's

181

custody. "The state must protect those it throws into snake pits, but the state need not guarantee that volunteer snake charmers will not be bitten," said one court.[6]

If the state has no constitutional duty to provide a safe workplace, it does have such a duty under occupational safety and health laws and regulations, which may be enforced either by federal or state agencies. Under the federal Occupational Safety and Health Act (OSHA), an employer has the general duty to keep the workplace free of recognized hazards that are likely to cause death or serious injury. Many states have similar laws.

In Oregon, the corrections department was fined by the state's accident prevention division for inadequately training correctional officers and not providing enough armed help for them in emergencies. In Washington State, the corrections department was ordered to provide bulletproof vests for parole officers.[7]

While a safety-related complaint made to a state regulatory agency may not be as dramatic as filing a lawsuit in federal court, these agencies may prove to be a faster, more effective remedy than federal court.

Environmental Issues

Correctional facilities, like other public and private enterprises, must comply with the various local, state, and federal environmental laws and regulations that have been adopted over the last several years. These include writing environmental-impact statements for new institutions, handling litigation over the siting of new facilities (which may be opposed by people on environmental grounds as well as on other grounds), disposing of sewage and garbage, using water and water quality, and a variety of other issues.

Environmental legal issues may or may not affect officers directly. In some cases, they directly may involve safety in the workplace, such as where an agency is required to remove asbestos from an institution. Other situations, such as where a facility can be located and what it must do to comply with sewage disposal rules, may be decided before a facility is built or has staff.

Other Statutory Rights

Various other federal laws include protections for correctional employees. Among these are the Fair Labor Standards Act (FLSA) and the Family Medical Leave Act (FMLA).

The Fair Labor Standards Act deals primarily with when an employer must pay overtime. The statute and accompanying regulations adopted by the U.S. Department of Labor are very complex. The basic principle of the law is that an employee is entitled to overtime pay (one and a half times regular pay) whenever the employee works more than forty hours per week. In some circumstances, compensatory time may be given instead of overtime pay. For most correctional officers, the need for overtime is not computed on the basis of a forty hour work week, but instead by looking at hours worked over a longer work period, which may range from seven to twenty-eight days.

The Family Medical Leave Act generally gives employees the right to take leave (which may be unpaid) for medical reasons, for the birth or adoption of a child, and to care for a sick spouse, child, or parent. As with the Fair Labor Standards Act, this is a complicated law, with a variety of limitations and restrictions.

Privacy Issues

In Chapter 7, we examined the rights of inmates to be free from unreasonable searches and seizures. The right comes from the Fourth Amendment. Officers also are protected by the Fourth Amendment, and the courts will take the same approach to analyzing an officer's search case as is used in an inmate's search case: The court will balance the needs of the institution for the particular type of search against the reasonable expectations of privacy that the officer enjoys.

In general, the officer enjoys a greater expectation of privacy than does the inmate. However, this expectation is not as great as it would be outside the institution. By choosing to work in a setting where security is very important, the officer's rights under the Fourth Amendment are reduced somewhat from what they would be on the street.

As long as searches are for work-related, administrative purposes (and not for criminal purposes), the Fourth Amendment's normal requirements of probable cause and search warrants do not apply to employment searches. Depending on the justification for the search and its intrusion, such work-related searches may require reasonable suspicion or, in some cases, may be done randomly.[8]

Thus, the institution may search purses and briefcases of staff coming into the facility, may pat search staff, and require them to pass magnetometer searches without any specific cause or suspicion. Yet, the institution must have reasonable suspicion to require the officer to submit to a strip search. Officer's vehicles may be subject to search, at least if they are parked on institution grounds where inmates would have access to them.[9]

To some extent, institution rules and policies are relevant in deciding if an employee has a reasonable expectation of privacy that might limit the types of searches the institution may be able to conduct legally. For instance, if institution rules and practices clearly indicate lockers are subject to search without cause, a court is more likely to approve random locker searches than if the employees are given the impression—both through policy and actual practice—that their lockers are their own property and are not subject to search absent some level of cause.

Random Urine Testing

The combination of increased drug usage among the general public and the development of reliable means of urine testing for drugs produced controversy and litigation during the 1980s. For staff, the question was under what circumstances, if any, an employer could randomly test employees or job applicants for drug usage.

The Supreme Court decided two cases in 1989 that said that in at least some circumstances, urine testing could be done without any particularized cause or suspicion that the employee had been using drugs.[10] From these cases, other courts now generally have ruled that random testing of employees whose jobs are particularly concerned with such things as public safety may be required without violating the Fourth Amendment. Correctional officers who have direct contact with inmates are among those courts have approved for random testing.[11] Although testing itself has been approved, there still may be concerns with such issues as the amount of privacy afforded the officer when actually providing the urine sample. Labor agreements may limit an employer's ability to implement a urine testing program, since the program may be something that must be bargained for with the union.

A Fall 2009 survey in the *Corrections Compendium* showed at least forty-three prison systems had employee drug testing programs, and twenty-five of these used random testing for permanent employees. Overall, the percentage of officers testing positive is extremely minimal. Only in Pennslyvania, New Hampshire, and West Virginia did more than 20 percent test positive for drugs. Arizona is the only reporting system that uses dogs for drug searches on an established schedule. Administrative staff are tested for substance abuse by thirty-one of the reporting systems.

Polygraph Tests

Federal law and regulations impose strict limitations on the use of polygraphs (lie detector tests) by private sector employers, but do not limit use of polygraphs by public sector employers such as state or local governments. However, many states have laws restricting or sometimes prohibiting the use of lie detectors. Even if the use of a polygraph might not violate the Constitution, it easily could violate state law. A Maryland jury awarded $900,000 in compensatory damages plus $4.1 million in punitive damages to four employees who were wrongfully fired for refusing to take a polygraph test.[13]

Even where state law permits an employer to require an employee to take a polygraph examination, courts may prohibit use of the results in either an administrative hearing or in a court proceeding. Use of polygraphs as well as other sometimes controversial means of testing are sometimes used in screening applicants for correctional jobs. Since correctional employers, like other employers, are sued from time to time by someone claiming to have been injured in some way by an employee the employer negligently hired, it is easy to understand why many employers are using an increased number of tools to try to screen prospective employees very carefully.

In a 1988 decision, the Third Circuit Court of Appeals refused to find that a polygraph test for prospective correctional employees violated either the due process or equal protection rights of the would-be employees.[14] The court made its decision less on a belief that the polygraph was highly accurate than because it could find no constitutional interest the job applicants had in the jobs for which they were applying. So, while polygraph results may not be used as part of the evidence to fire someone, they may be used as part of the decision to hire the person in the first place. Agency personnel policies should address under what circumstances, if at all, an employee or prospective employee may be required to take a polygraph test.

Confidential Information

An employer may be able to obtain a substantial amount of personal information about an employee. This might include information such as drug usage, medical conditions, prior criminal history, participation in counseling, and so forth. While the employer may have a legitimate reason for knowing this confidential information, that does not entitle the employer to release that information to people who have no reason to know it. This can include the general public and other employees.

Where private facts about an employee are improperly released, the employee may be able to successfully sue for invasion of privacy. In general, when an employer has information the reasonable person would consider private, the employer should have a legitimate business reason for disclosing that information even within the organization. Protecting confidential information becomes particularly important for information that can be particularly embarrassing and potentially damaging to the employee. This would include information about an employee's drug use and about employees who might be HIV positive or have AIDS.

Due Process and Employee Discipline

For many years, it was assumed that the typical civil service employee disciplinary hearing provided all the due process necessary to terminate an employee. Usually these procedures included a full hearing, which occurred sometime after the employee actually was terminated. If the employee won the hearing, the relief could include not only reinstatement but also payment of lost wages.

In 1985, the Supreme Court looked at the question of what sort of due process protections the government employee had and whether a post-termination hearing under state civil service laws was sufficient. In the case of *Cleveland Board of Education v. Loudermill*,[15] the Court decided a post-termination hearing alone did not provide the employee with due process. Instead, the Fourteenth Amendment required a limited pre-termination hearing in addition to whatever hearing rights the employee might have after the termination.

The pre-termination hearing, the Court said, is not to resolve the propriety of the decision to fire the employee. It is only to serve as a check against mistakes and to decide if there are reasonable grounds to believe the charges against the employee are true. Therefore, the hearing required by the *Loudermill* case is quite simple and informal. The employee must be given either written or oral notice of the charges. The employer must give an explanation of the evidence against the employee, who must have a chance to present his or her side of the case.

Conclusion

When employees feel their concerns and problems are not being addressed adequately by the employer, they increasingly are willing to take those concerns to court. In contrast to inmates, who are largely limited to raising claims under the Constitution, there are several different legal vehicles that employees may use to protect and advance their interests.

Review Questions

1. List three sources of officers' rights.

2. True or False: While sexual discrimination is against the law, sexual harassment is not.

3. True or False: Courts consistently have ruled that random urine testing of correctional officers is an unreasonable search.

Endnotes

[1] *Price Waterhouse v. Hopkins*, 109 S.Ct. 1775 (1989).

[2] *Ward's Cove Packing v. Atonio*, 109 S.Ct. 2115 (1989).

[3] *Johnson v. Transportation Agency*, Santa Clara County, 107 S.Ct. 1442 (1987).

[4] *U.S. v. Paradise*, 107 S.Ct. 1053 (1987).

[5] *Hammer v. King County*, W.D. No. C89-521R.

[6] *Walker v. Rowe*, 791 F.2d 507, 511 (7th Cir., 1986). *Washington v. District of Columbia*, 802 F.2d 1478 (D.C. Cir., 1986).

[7] Collins, W, 1987. *Correctional Law.* (Self-published). p. 109.

[8] *O'Connor v. Ortega*, 107 S.Ct. 1492 (1987).

[9] *McDonnell v. Hunter* 809 F.2d 1302 (8th Cir., 1987).

[10] *Skinner v. Railway Labor Executives' Association*, 109 S.Ct. 1402 (1989); *National Treasury Employees Union v. Von Raab*, 109 S.Ct. 1378 (1989).

[11] *Taylor v. O'Grady*, 888 F.2d 1189 (7th Cir., 1989).

[12.] *Employee Drug-Testing Policies In Prison Systems*, National Institute of Justice, Research in Action, August 1988.

[13.] *Monlodis v. Cook*, 494 A.2d 212 (Md. Ct. Spec. App., 1984).

[14.] *Anderson v. City of Philadelphia*, 845 F.2d 1216 (3rd Cir., 1988).

[15.] *Cleveland Board of Education v. Loudermill*, 105 S.Ct. 1487 (1985).

Chapter 14:
The Americans with
Disabilities Act (ADA)

In 1990, Congress passed the Americans with Disabilities Act (ADA). This law, described as the "Bill of Rights" for the disabled, prohibits discrimination against people with disabilities in employment, public services and transportation, public accommodations, and telecommunications. For purposes of those working in corrections, the portions of ADA dealing with employment and government services are probably of the greatest importance.

ADA provides protections for people applying for work and working in corrections, as well as for inmates (who are recipients of "government services, programs, or activities").[1] The ADA also provides protections to other people entering the correctional institution, such as visitors, who also would be seen as participants in or recipients of government services or programs.

The goal of the ADA is to provide a truly equal opportunity for disabled persons to participate in employment and government programs. To do this will require changes in the way employment decisions are made, the way buildings are built, and the way programs are run. For instance, a mobility-impaired person may be able to perform a particular job as well as someone who is fully mobile, except for the fact that the job site is up a flight of stairs that the person cannot climb. To provide the disabled person with an equal opportunity, that physical barrier may have to be removed.

ADA's prohibitions against discrimination are not absolute. In general, a person who is disabled must be "otherwise qualified" to perform the job or participate in a government program or activity. The employer or government service provider must make reasonable accommodations to allow the disabled person to participate, but if the alterations of the job or program would be too great, the individual need not be accommodated. So, the general duty the law creates not to discriminate has limits.

"Disability" is broadly defined under the ADA to include the following:

- A physical or mental impairment that substantially limits one or more of the major life activities of such individual

- A record of such impairment

- Being regarded as having such an impairment

While some may think of ADA as only requiring physical alterations to buildings through such things as ramps, wheelchair lifts, and the like, ADA requires far more than just making a building physically accessible to people in wheelchairs or on crutches. For instance, ADA may require accommodating people with mental disabilities (such as learning disabilities) by making changes in the amount of reading a job or program requires.

While "legitimate penological interests" may permit a correctional institution to restrict the constitutional rights of an inmate (*see* Chapter 5), ADA imposes a greater burden on the agency discriminating against a person with a disability to justify that discrimination and avoid accommodating the person's disability in some way. For instance, the employer has a duty to accommodate the otherwise qualified employee with a disability up to the point of the employer incurring an "undue hardship." An undue hardship might be shown if an accommodation were unduly costly, extensive, disruptive, or would fundamentally alter the nature of the operation or business. Note, these are subjective determinations, which will vary from one setting to another. Similar burdens exist to justify denying access to a government program or service. Detailed federal regulations flesh out and interpret the statutory requirements of the ADA.[2]

Federal appeals courts are split on the question of whether institutional security concerns can validly justify discriminating against disabled inmates under the ADA and whether the "*Turner* test" (*see* Chapter 5) can be used to evaluate this type of issue.[3]

In the *Gates* case, HIV-positive inmates protested being barred from being allowed to work in prison food services. They argued that the bar violated their rights under the ADA. Officials said their decision was based not on a fear that HIV would be transmitted by the inmates, but rather in response to threats of disturbances from other inmates. The district court ruled in favor of the HIV-positive inmates, but the court of appeals reversed, holding that legitimate security needs of the prison justified the exclusion, even though neither the ADA nor its regulations recognize security concerns as a basis for discriminating against a person. The court simply created a new exception to the law. Should courts follow the *Gates* approach, it could substantially limit the application of the ADA in many prison settings.

The same issue came before the 11th Circuit Court of Appeals. In a 1997 decision by a three-judge panel, the court refused to follow the *Gates* approach, saying it was more appropriate for Congress to adopt major exceptions to normal ADA requirements than for courts to create such exceptions.[4] But a year later, the court vacated its 1997 holding pending an en banc review by the entire court. In 1999, the court held that the district court's reliance on the four *Turner* factors to support its decision in favor of the institution was acceptable.[5] In the 1997 decision, the court specifically discussed and criticized the *Gates* decision but two years later, it did not even mention it.

Despite the obvious importance of the question about whether the *Turner* test is relevant in ADA cases, other circuits have not yet clearly addressed the question.

Endnotes

[1] In *Pennsylvania Department of Corrections v. Yeskey*, 524 U.S. 206, 118 S.Ct. 1952, 141 L.Ed.2d 215 (1998), the Supreme Court held specifically that the ADA extends to and protects inmates.

[2] *See* 28 CFR Parts 25 and 29, CFR Part 1630. The ADA appears at 42 USC Sec. 12020, et. seq.

[3] *Gates v. Rowland*, 39 F.3d 1439 (9th Cir., 1994) applied the *Turner* test.

[4] *Onishea v. Hopper*, 126 F.3d 1323 (11th Cir., 1997).

[5] *Onishea v. Hopper*, 171 F.3d 1289 (11th Cir., 1999).

Answers to Review Questions

Chapter 1:

There are no review questions for Chapter 1.

Chapter 2:

1. The three periods or eras of court involvement with corrections were the hands-off era, the hands-on era, and the one-hand-on, one-hand-off era.

2. Two factors that led to the courts first becoming involved with correctional issues included the civil rights movement and poor correctional practices involving prisoners' rights on health care, treatment by correctional staff, and the overall quality of life while in prison.

3. In passing the Prison Litigation Reform Act, Congress attempted to make it more difficult for inmates to file civil rights law suits in federal courts to limit the power of the federal court in ordering relief in inmate rights' cases.

4. The Supreme Court requires lower courts to show increased deference to the judgment of correctional officers and administrators.

Chapter 3:

1. The three types of lawsuits most commonly filed by inmates are civil rights action (42 USC Sec. 1983), habeas corpus actions, and tort suits.

2. True. A state cannot be sued directly in a civil rights action. Under 42 USC Sec. 1983, the suit must be against a "person," and the state is not a person.

3. An example of when a supervisor could be held liable in a civil rights action, even if the supervisor did not take part directly in the actions that led to the suit occurs in a "failure-to-supervise" case. If a supervisor is aware of the constitutionally offensive acts done to an inmate by another staff member, and fails to take action to correct the situation, then the supervisor is liable by his or her inaction to take remedial steps. Failure to train officers properly in constitutionally sensitive areas also could be the basis of supervisory liability.

Chapter 4:

1. The right of access to the courts is an important part of America's legal system. Without the courts or some similar dispute-resolving body with the power to enforce its decisions, rights would belong only to the strongest, and any freedoms "guaranteed" by laws or the Constitution would become futile if they are not enforced by a governing body.

2. If an inmate is represented by appointed counsel in a criminal case, this is not necessarily sufficient access-to-the-courts because appointed counsel often do not offer "meaningful access to the courts" (as stipulated by the *Bounds* case) because they are unable to provide the inmate with any advice or assistance outside of the criminal case. Furthermore, once inmates are sentenced to jail or prison, they are no longer represented by that counsel.

3. The major vulnerability of access-to-the-courts system, which is built around books and other written materials, is access for the inmate with limited reading skills as well as the inmate who has limited English-language skills.

Chapter 5:

1. The most common institutional concern that may justify restriction of an inmate's constitutional rights is the security of the institution.

2. False. The *Turner* test has made it easier for an institution to justify restricting constitutional rights of inmates.

3. The institution will lose on restricting an inmate's practice of his or her religion. To win, the institution must explain in at least some detail why the restriction is related to security. The statement "The restriction was imposed because of security needs" is too vague; it lacks a valid argument backed by factual evidence.

Chapter 6:

1. The most common justification for restricting inmates' First Amendment rights' is security of the institution.

2. The major difference between the legal test imposed by the First Amendment for evaluation of a restriction on an inmate's ability to practice his or

her religion and the legal test imposed by the Religious Land Use and Institutionalized Persons Act is that the test under RLUIPA is more difficult. It reduces the level of deference courts can give to judgments of correctional administrators and increases the power of the courts to second guess such decisions by imposing a requirement that restrictions on religious practices be the "least-restrictive" alternative.

3. Since the beginning of the twenty-first century, the Supreme Court has not stepped back from its long-held position that lower courts must give substantial deference to judgment calls of correctional officials about such things as institutional safety and security. The Court reemphasized the importance of deference in its 2003 case on visiting, *Bazzetta v. Overton.*

Chapter 7:

1. Even though the Supreme Court has held that inmates have no expectation of privacy in regard to their cells, a cell search might trigger court intervention if the cell was left in complete disarray after the search. If the cell appeared messy or in shambles after the search, then the search was seen as conducted in an unreasonable manor.

2. To justify visitor strip searches, there must be reasonable suspicion that the visitor is hiding contraband on his or her person.

3. The most important thing for correctional officers to remember when performing an inmate search is to maintain a high level of professionalism at all times. It is imperative to respect the dignity of the inmates while doing searches.

Chapter 8:

1. It is the responsibility of the correctional medical staff to make the decision concerning whether an inmate needs medical care. The extent of the medical decisions that custody staff may make are allowing inmates to contact medical staff at any given point during the day or night.

2. The general areas a court will focus on in a conditions-of-confinement suit include basic human needs: personal safety, medical care, sanitation, food service, shelter, and clothing.

3. Crowding is an important issue in conditions-of-confinement suits because crowding often results in a breakdown of a facility's ability to provide the inmates with their basic human needs.

Chapter 9:

1. Two types of legal actions that could be brought following a suicide (or suicide attempt) by the survivors of the deceased include:

    a. A civil rights action (claiming a violation of a constitutional right) and

    b. A tort suit (claiming negligence).

2. The three factual claims most likely to appear in a suicide case include:

    a. Failure to identify a potentially suicidal inmate,

    b. Failure to monitor a potentially suicidal inmate once he or she is identified as being suicidal, and

    c. Failure to properly respond to a suicide attempt once it is discovered.

3. Two examples of where an individual officer's failures could provide the basis for a suicide lawsuit include:

    a. Failure to complete a suicide-screening questionnaire at booking and

    b. Failure to monitor an inmate according to policy (ten-minute checks, fifteen-minute checks, and so forth).

Chapter 10:

1. Deadly force may not be used to protect property. Deadly force may only be used in self-defense and in the protection of others from death or serious bodily harm and, in at least some cases, in the prevention of escape.

2. In a constitutional excess force case, the five questions a court will ask include:

    a. What was the need for force?

    b. What was the amount of force used?

    c. What injuries were sustained by the inmate.

    d. What was the threat perceived by the reasonable correctional officer?

    e. What efforts to temper the use of force did the officer make?

3. Detailed use-of-force reports are important to include for the following reasons:

   a. They allow the supervisor to evaluate the use-of-force incident.

   b. They allow a court to evaluate the use-of-force incident.

   c. They allow the officer to review the details of the incident prior to testifying.

   d. They may be able to be introduced into evidence at a trial.

Chapter 11:

1. There are more procedural rights in a parole-revocation hearing than in a prison or jail disciplinary hearing because parole is seen as a form of conditional liberty, which means that there is more to potentially lose in a parole revocation than there is for an inmate who is already in custody and does not have such conditional liberties at that point in time.

2. Procedural due process focuses on how the courts go about making the decision to take away life, liberty, or property, such as in disciplinary hearings. The state is required to go through certain steps in making such decisions, which usually involve notice to the person of the proposed deprivation and some form of a hearing. Substantive due process, on the other hand, focuses on what the final decision is, not just the process of getting there. The main area in corrections where substantive due process is important is in litigation regarding the conditions of confinement of pretrial detainees. Another example of substantive due process includes the grounds necessary to involuntarily medicate an inmate.

3. The hearing officer may rely on evidence from a witness whose identity is not disclosed to the inmate charged with the offense when the hearing officer can be convinced the informant is reliable by a corrections officer who knows the identity of the informant. However, unless the informant was an eyewitness to the incident, the information is suspect; therefore, the hearing officer must decide if the information is or is not believable both in light of the nature of the information itself and its source.

Chapter 12:

1. An agency is likely to refuse to defend an employee sued by an inmate when the employee acts outside the scope of his or her duties and in bad faith.

2. Types of discovery include:

   a. Depositions

   b. Interrogatories

   c. Motions to produce, and

   d. Requests for admissions.

3. When testifying, witnesses should not try to memorize answers to the lawyer's questions.

Chapter 13:

1. Sources of officers' rights include:

   a. Union contracts

   b. Civil service laws

   c. Discrimination laws

   d. Occupational health and safety laws, and

   e. State and federal constitutional law.

2. False. While sexual discrimination is against the law, sexual harassment is also against the law as it is a form of sexual discrimination.

3. False. Courts have not consistently ruled that random urine testing of correctional officers is an unreasonable search; decisions are mixed as to whether correctional officers may be subject to random urine testing.

Chapter 14.

There are no review questions for Chapter 14.

Index

T

U

Y

About the Author

William C. Collins is an attorney and consultant in Olympia, Washington, specializing in correctional law. A former director of ACA's Correctional Law Project, he is the coeditor and cofounder of the *Correctional Law Reporter*, a bimonthly journal that reviews and discusses legal issues and developments in corrections. Mr. Collins has provided legal issues training in thirty-five states and has published several books dealing with correctional law as well as numerous articles. Before entering private practice, he worked with the Washington State Attorney General's Office as the first head of their corrections division. With more than three decades of experience, he is generally recognized as one of the country's most knowledgeable attorneys in the correctional field.